Contents

Personal possessions are salvaged from Wellington Road, Aberdeen

ABERDEEN

and the North-East at War

BERNARD BALE

BLACK & WHITE PUBLISHING

First published 2005
by Black & White Publishing Ltd,
99 Giles Street, Edinburgh EH6 6BZ

ISBN 184502 0731

British Library Cataloguing in publication data: a catalogue record for
this book is available from The British Library.

The photographs drawn from The Press and Journal archives can be purchased from the
Photosales Department Tel: 01224 338011, or by visiting www.weescottishphotos.com.

Acknowledgements: Assistance given with the newspaper articles and picture research:
Duncan Smith and Robert Stewart, The Press and Journal; Aberdeen Library and Information Services.

Printed and bound in Poland
www.polskabook.pl

INTRODUCTION

Throughout history Britain has been at war with various nations for various reasons and always at the forefront of the engagements there have been troops, sailors and, during the last century, pilots from the north-east. There have been times when the Scots have been at war with the English and even with fellow Scots. Perhaps it is because Scots are natural warriors that they have never been at peace for very long.

This is a tribute to heroes of World War Two from Aberdeen and the north-east, some named and some un-named but it is more than even that because it is also a tribute to those men, women and children who bravely lived through one of the darkest times of civilised man. While there were those at the sharp end, at home there were the land girls, the evacuees and those taking care of them, the firemen, the mums keeping the kids secure while the dads were away with a rifle in their hand.

Nobody could live through such an experience as World War Two without having a tale to tell. In this book we touch on just a small number of those tales during what was the best of times and the worst of times.

Many more stories lie beneath the surface but hopefully this will in some way celebrate all of those who endured the time between 1939 and 1945 when, along with the rest of the world, Aberdeen and the north-east was at war.

THE EARLY YEARS

THE DAY THAT WAR BROKE OUT

All over the country people gathered round their wireless sets. Streets were deserted. News bulletins had been bringing information from Europe, information which confirmed what many had been saying for months and even years. Germany was on the march and the worst nightmare was being realised, a return to conflict in Europe, a return to the horrors of World War One, horrors which were still so vivid in the memories of families left in mourning after the war to end all wars.

Germany's invasion of Poland was the final blow. In the early hours of Friday, September 1, 1939, German troops had swept into Poland amid protests from much of the rest of Europe. The British voice was among the loudest of those protestors. No response came from Adolf Hitler other than to continue the course he had chosen.

Thus it was that Britain came to a standstill on the morning of September 3. A simple radio announcement at 11 am broadcast the message that the Prime Minister, Neville Chamberlain, would address the nation at 11.15. The word spread very quickly and traffic came to a halt in Glasgow, Edinburgh, Aberdeen, Dundee and every other Scottish city, town and village. Farmers stopped their work, hospitals became more silent than before and all around the coast, boats bobbed at their moorings as an eerie hush fell over the country. It was the only time that Hitler would succeed in bringing Britain to a standstill.

The voice of Neville Chamberlain sounded nervous and tired. He revealed that the British government had sought an undertaking from the German government that German troops would withdraw from Poland. A time limit had been imposed.

"I have to tell you now that no such undertaking has been received and consequently this country is at war with Germany," said the Prime Minister.

It was the worst possible news. Another war, more death and destruction. But Hitler could not be allowed to get away with it. Who knew where he might invade next? An invasion of Britain could not be ruled out and the thought of German jackboots stamping down the heather, raised the hackles of the people of Scotland.

Britain was prepared but perhaps not as well as she might have been. Some politicians had been warning that Hitler had been strengthening his forces and hurriedly building up his arsenal but their prophesies had largely fallen on deaf ears amid accusations of scaremongering.

Gas masks had been issued months earlier just in case there was a sudden strike from the

Bomb damage to Peterhead Academy

maverick German chancellor and leaflets had been put through the nation's letterboxes giving information on defence procedures and facilities. As soon as war was declared, millions of Anderson shelters were distributed throughout the nation but, while the armour had been checked, the armoury was still lacking.

It was helpful then that Hitler was so busy on the first phase of his quest for world domination that Britain had little involvement for the first weeks of conflict. On the day that Neville Chamberlain had announced that we were at war, Australia, New Zealand and other Commonwealth countries pledged their allegiance by also declaring themselves at war with Germany. Later in the day France also declared themselves at war with Germany and the troops of other nations were put on red alert as everyone waited for the lit fuse to reach the powder keg.

Perhaps the first real danger came from the blackout which had been warned of before and came into play as soon as war had been declared. Thick black material became curtains, black paint and painted wood or cardboard panels ensured that not a glimmer of light escaped from windows to help the German bombers which would surely prowl the skies looking for targets.

The blackout had its own dangers though and during its early days there was a sharp rise in road accidents with deaths from those accidents doubling. Glasgow also had a sharp rise in twisted ankles as people tripped over kerb stones and each other.

People were encouraged to wear something white and shops ran out of white raincoats and other clothing. Many men started to walk around with their shirt tails hanging out of their trousers.

A speed limit of 20 mph was imposed during blackout periods and white lines were painted on kerb stones and lamp posts to help prevent more accidents. Trains continued to run, although more slowly, and the carriages were lit by dim blue lights.

If nothing else, these measures served to unite the population since the precautions affected everyone whether bank manager, doctor or market trader. The blackout also proved to be a good way of meeting people and more than one romance began as a result of people going bump in the night.

Evacuation was high on the agenda of war priorities and there were many culture shocks as city-dwelling youngsters were taken into the country. Some of the gentry found themselves wielding nit combs for the first time and some of the urban kids breathed fresh air for the first time. It was a meeting of two worlds and while there were many happy tales afterwards, there were also many sighs of relief when it was all over.

Away from these shores British troops were already in action, helping to stem the flow of the German military machine into other countries and there was a hunger at home for wireless and newspaper bulletins although the reports only ever gave a sketchy account of the reality.

A recruitment drive at Albert Quay, Aberdeen

Nothing is spared as these ornamental railings are taken from the graves for the war effort

Opinions were exchanged all day about how long the war would last. The previous major conflict had been an endurance test lasting four years. Optimists proclaimed that it would all be over within a year because the Germans would extend themselves too far too quickly. The pessimists could see no end to the hostility and anticipated that peace had gone forever since there would be outbreaks of conflict every few years, pointing to the First World War as just the beginning.

The war clouds spread gloom over Britain but there was a resolve too and nowhere was it stronger than north of the border where the Scottish regiments had been the backbone of the British army for centuries and those who remained at home had that same gritty determination that no aggressor would prevail, least of all Adolf Hitler and his German military machine. It might roll over Europe but it would never crush Scottish spirit.

AIR RAIDS

When the sirens wailed, conversations ceased and hearts sank as people fled to the shelters or simply hid under their tables hoping that a mattress might cushion them from any devastation caused by any landing bombs.

There is little doubt that Coventry, London's East End and many other cities suffered wholesale destruction as Hitler tried to bring Britain to its knees. It was Edinburgh that was first into the front line though on the afternoon of October 16, 1939 when a German aircraft roared over the city.

The sirens had not sounded so this was no bombing invasion but it was an attack nevertheless on an unsuspecting target - naval vessels moored near the Forth Bridge. The *Press and Journal* carried a report at the time which gave this account by an unnamed correspondent.

"The sight of a huge aeroplane zooming close over the housetops of Inverkeithing, Fife, with flames and smoke trailing behind it, will always remain one of my most vivid and thrilling memories of the Germans' first bomber raid on Britain.

"The plane seemed to just clear the houses. It was so near that the iron crosses on the body and swastikas under the wings could be plainly seen.

"Though on fire and out of control, swaying dangerously from side to side, the bomber was still making a fight. I could hear its machine gun spluttering. It disappeared eastwards, falling lower and lower and crashed to earth somewhere beyond.

"That plane falling to destruction was practically the first intimation that I and many others had of this amazing raid which cost the lives of 16 and injury to 44 men of the navy in addition to civil casualties. Enemy losses are variously stated at from four to seven machines.

"This awakening to reality was thus rude and complete. Before me stretched the waters

Gas masks were vital for everyone

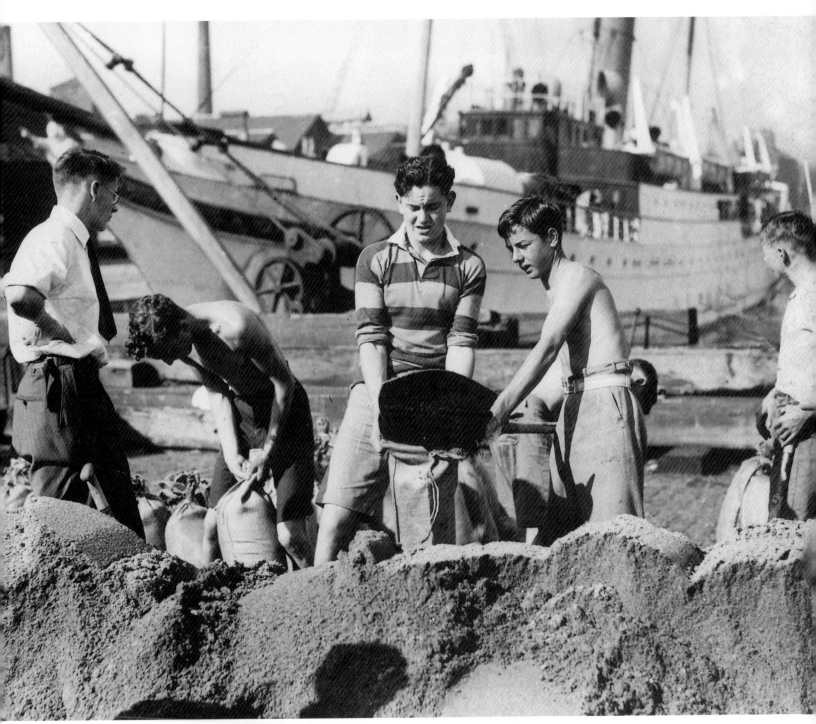

Robert Gordon's College boys filled more than their minds. Here they are filling sandbags

A telephone exchange during a gas mask drill

of the Forth, calm and blue, with the towering spans of the great bridge over which a train was actually passing.

"So the first stage of the raid was over before people began to understand that a raid was on at all for it was made in two stages.

"The first stage opened with the appearance of a solitary plane which came from the direction of Edinburgh city, flying lower as it approached. Passing over the bridge it suddenly dived towards the vessels lying at anchor there and then a bomb streaked downwards dropping close to one of the ships and exploding with a shattering crash.

"Following the disappearance of the plane, the all-clear signal was sounded at South Queensferry. The siren had scarcely ceased when out of the blue came three other raiders roaring down at the ships.

"Again the bombs kissed their targets and the roar of the explosions mingled with a spirited fire from the anti-aircraft guns on the vessels. The batteries on shore joined in. It was one of those planes which passed close over Inverkeithing to crash in flames.

"It was the first raider to fall but not the first to give best to the defenders. What I did not learn until later was that exactly five minutes earlier, two enemy planes which had chosen to approach up the Firth of Forth had been intercepted by RAF fighting machines near the May Island. After a hot engagement they had been driven down to within a few feet of the water and chased out to sea.

"The rattle of machine guns told that our fighters had entered into the combat though they could not always get at close-quarters owing to the anti-aircraft shells that were being peppered around their quarry. They were always on the raiders' tails however and were responsible for the fact that the fate of the machine I had seen crash was shared by three more at least.

"A train, delayed at Dalmeny, had been allowed to proceed across the bridge when the raid was thought to have finished. Of what immediately followed, the passengers had a 'front seat view'.

"One Aberdeen man on the train told me: 'I had gone into the corridor to get a good view of the naval vessels. When we were about the middle of the bridge I saw a great explosion in the water behind one of the ships. I had just yelled a warning to the other passengers when another explosion occurred on a pinnace lying alongside a cruiser. It was a direct hit on the little craft. The next moment we could see nothing but wreckage.

"'A third explosion occurred near a cruiser but so far I could see no damage was done to the warships. It was now we saw the German planes. The nearest one was a red machine that flew within a couple of hundred yards of where we stood. It seemed to be rather lower than the top of the bridge.

"'Anti-aircraft guns started firing and I could see that one of the planes was hit. A couple

Bomb damage at Forbesfield Road. This was one of the first – and one of the very few – pictures of bomb damage in Aberdeen published during the war

Mustang III of No 65 "East India" Squadron pictured at Peterhead RAF Station, 1945

612 County of Aberdeen Squadron Auxiliary Air Force at Dyce

Snug and safe in James Christie's do-it-yourself air raid shelter.

Survivors of an August 1941 raid on Peterhead clutch salvaged possessions. Mrs Cooke (centre of group) just managed to reach the shelter as the bomb burst

of men in the next compartment told me they had seen this machine crash in a field.

"'In the meantime our train had slowed down and in the excitement we did not realise our own danger. If a plane or bomb had hit the bridge we would all have perished.'

"Thus it was that Scotland experienced its first air attack."

There were other reports of initial bombing activity with claims that the first German bomb to land on British soil was in Shetland while others have claimed that it actually fell on Hoy in Orkney. Whatever is true, there is no account so vivid as the rain on the naval ships at the Forth Bridge, a clear indication that hostilities were well and truly underway.

A home-made air raid shelter in Peterhead

Gas mask distribution to children just before the outbreak of war

FIRST SHOT AT SEA

Even as war was declared there was an attack at sea which captured the headlines and immediately set pulses racing on both sides of the Atlantic.

The *Athenia* was one of the few ships allowed to sail from Europe as the announcement of war was days away. People were frantic to get to the US. Therefore the small *Anchor-Donaldson* liner was filled way beyond capacity. It was a warm September day when she left Glasgow with her first complement on September 1st. She then sailed to Belfast and many gathered on deck for an emotional church service which included the hymn 'For Those in Peril on the Sea'.

Finally on September 2, the ship stopped at Liverpool where British school children carried boxes with gas masks in them as they made their way to the dockside.

The *Athenia* then made her way to the open sea with about 1400 passengers, mostly women and children.

While at sea, it was announced that news of war was official.

As the red sun slowly dipped into the sea, the German submarine *U-30* crept closer and closer to her target.

With a large jolt and without any warning whatsoever, the *Athenia* was struck by a torpedo. Captain Gaillard fought to keep the ship steady as his crew directed passengers to the lifeboats, an inadequate number of lifeboats for the overcrowded ship.

The climb to the lifeboats was perilous as the stern slowly settled into the choppy sea. Many families were parted due to over crowding. One survivor noticed a heavy dusting of powder that came from the shelling as she and others milled about the decks trying to find a lifeboat. The sun disappeared and darkness covered the ocean.

It was alleged that the U-boat surfaced to witness the mayhem that followed and actually fired shells at survivors before disappearing once again into the depths of the ocean.

As the lifeboats rowed away, some were so old they were damaged in the lowering and survivors bailed continuously.

The *Athenia* although settling, seemed to be all right to those who slowly drifted into the night.

Finally help arrived, but unfortunately for some, it was the cause of their demise. Two lifeboats were destroyed trying to board the rescue vessels.

All in all, 112 people were killed. 69 of them were women and children. 15 hours after being struck by the torpedo, the *Athenia* sank from view.

The news was greeted with horror on both sides of the Atlantic and around the rest of the world. Anyone who was left in any doubt about Germany's intentions was blown off the fence and forced to realise that Hitler was on a course of ruthlessness and had to be stopped.

Ratings crowd the deck on the occasion of the official visit to HMS Scylla

The Royal Naval escort ship HMS Aberdeen which was launched in 1936

*A type VIIc U-boat – U-766
– in Aberdeen Harbour*

Press and Journal

Light Up: 8.59 p.m. Lights Out: 5.15 a.m.

No. 26,420, 192nd Year   ABERDEEN, MONDAY, SEPTEMBER 4, 1939   ONE PENNY

FIVE NATIONS AT WAR WITH GERMANY

HITLER REFUSES TO WITHDRAW

King Calls to His People and the Empire Rallies

LORD GORT AS SUPREME C.-IN-C. OF BRITISH FIELD FORCES

From 11 a.m. yesterday Britain and Germany were at war. At 5 p.m. France's ultimatum to the Reich expired.

GERMANY REPLIED TO BRITAIN'S FINAL WARNING TWENTY MINUTES AFTER THE TIME LIMIT HAD EXPIRED.

SHE REFUSED TO WITHDRAW FROM POLAND, AND SOUGHT TO PLACE THE BLAME FOR DEVELOPMENTS UPON BRITAIN.

WITH COMPOSURE AND RESOLUTION THE BRITISH GOVERNMENT AND PEOPLE HAVE PROCEEDED TO PUT NECESSARY MEASURES INTO OPERATION.

A WAR CABINET HAS BEEN FORMED. IT INCLUDES MR WINSTON CHURCHILL AS FIRST LORD OF THE ADMIRALTY. MR EDEN IS MADE DOMINIONS SECRETARY, AND IS TO HAVE SPECIAL ACCESS TO THE WAR CABINET.

Lord Gort was last night appointed Commander-in-Chief of the British Field Forces; General Sir Edmund Ironside, Chief of the Imperial General Staff; and General Sir Walter Kirke, Commander-in-Chief of the Home Forces.

KING TO HIS PEOPLE

The King last night broadcast a call to his people at home and abroad. He asked them "to stand calm and firm and united in this time of trial."

A copy of his message is to be sent to every home in the country. The Dominions are swiftly rallying to the side of the Motherland.

Australia and New Zealand have declared themselves at war, and Canada is placing her forces on a war footing. This means that five nations are now at war with Germany.

Sikander Hyat Khan, Premier of the Indian Province of Punjab, yesterday appealed to all Punjabis to do their duty "by King and country."

A NUMBER OF FINANCIAL MEASURES WERE ANNOUNCED DURING THE DAY. ALL BANKS WILL BE CLOSED TO-DAY, BUT THERE WILL BE NO GENERAL MORATORIUM DURING THE WAR.

A regulation issued requires every one to offer the bankers for sale their treasury and bullion foreign their

Press and Journal

Light Up: 8.59 p.m. Lights Out: 5.15 a.m.

ABERDEEN, MONDAY, SEPTEMBER 4, 1939

SCOTS LINER TORPEDOED
1400 ON BOARD

ATHENIA SINKING IN ATLANTIC

FIRST ACT IN WAR WITH GERMANY

King Calls to His People and the Empire Rallies

Norwegian fishing boats are 'repatriated'. They are seen here being loaded aboard a tank landing craft for transport to Norway

EVACUATION

As war fever gripped the nation, rural areas of Scotland braced themselves for an invasion of a different sort, the invasion of a friendly army of children and their mothers.

Thousands from Scotland's industrial and military zones were earmarked for private households in rural areas thought to be safe from the raids of the Luftwaffe.

The main concern was the safety of children and the government made evacuation a priority. In Scotland the danger zones were considered to be Edinburgh, Glasgow, Dundee, Clydebank and Rosyth although, ironically, it later turned out that Aberdeen was attacked by enemy planes 32 times, the largest number of attacks on any Scottish town.

On September 1, Aberdeen greeted 30,000 children of school age and 10,000 mothers with their infants. Reception areas were set up in towns and villages throughout the area with Drumoak receiving the first contingent of evacuees to arrive in Aberdeenshire.

Mothers were asked to try and ensure that each child had a gas mask, change of underclothing, night clothes, house shoes or rubber shoes, spare stockings, socks, toothbrush, towel, comb, handkerchief, warm coat or mackintosh, tin cup or mug.

Assembly points had been set up at primary schools in the various districts before the children were dispatched to the country in packed trains.

Mothers and fathers fought back tears as they parted with their children but for many of the youngsters themselves it seemed like the start of a great adventure and they eagerly clutched their teddy bears and toys in one hand and their gas masks in the other.

On reaching destinations the youngsters would find in many cases kindly foster parents who had bought in large stocks of sweets and comics. There were those though who found themselves in households that had never had nor ever wanted children to be present.

The transfer of the population did run into some snags. In Lanarkshire tempers flared with the arrival of 500 evacuees from Glasgow, their mothers protesting bitterly at suggestions that individual families would have to be split up.

There were other failures too. Mothers, unused to country life, headed home to their menfolk. Tragically, as the threat of air attack seemed to dwindle, many returned to Clydebank only to die in the bombing onslaught which reduced the bustling area to a smouldering graveyard in March 1941.

The first day of the evacuation exodus from Edinburgh brought a slow response from parents although news of the invasion of Poland soon changed minds.

Efforts were made to reimburse foster parents. In the case of unaccompanied children they received 10s 6d per week where one child was billeted. If more than one child was given a home they received 8s 6d per child. The money did not cover the cost of clothes or medical expenses though.

Reports also came in from some areas that unexpected problems had occurred when

Evacuees, doing their best to look cheerful, are never without their gas mask boxes

children born and bred in city life were let loose in the countryside. At Port Elphinstone an eight-year-old girl was drowned in a mill lade while a 16-year-old evacuee dived to rescue his pal from drowning in Macduff harbour.

For many of those children it was their first sight of a cow or a pig and they had no idea about closing gates.

Many elderly people were also evacuated, mostly under their own steam without any official direction from the government. They sought sanctuary from the bombs dropping on the cities and were reminded not to forget their pension books.

Perhaps the strangest evacuee was a pet canary which was sent by its loving owner from its home in the Midlands to Oban to be safe from the menace of the Luftwaffe.

The Royal Observer Corps headquaters at Woolmarhill. Personnel are wearing police arm bands

Press and Journal

Black-out Time 6 p.m.   Motor Lights Out: 7.46 a.m.

ABERDEEN, WEDNESDAY, OCTOBER 18, 1939

5 AIR RAIDS ON SCAPA FLOW

NAZIS LOSE FOUR MORE PLANES

BATTLESHIP IRON DUKE DAMAGED

NAZI GERMANY IS WAGING A DETERMINED AIR WAR ON BRITAIN, BUT AT GREAT COST.

Five separate air raids were carried out yesterday on Scapa Flow, and two bombs falling near the battleship Iron Duke caused certain damage.

Bombs fell on Orkney.   No one was injured.

Fourteen bombers took part in the raids, but they got such a hot reception from anti-aircraft guns that two of them were destroyed and another was believed to be damaged.

Press and Journal

Black-out Time: 5.35 p.m.   Motor Lights Out: 8 7 a.m.

No. 26,467, 192nd Year   ABERDEEN, SATURDAY, OCTOBER 28, 1939

LORD GORT SEES "JOCKS" AT FRONT

INSPECTS BILLETS AND TRENCHES

MEETS ABERDEEN LAD ON FIRESTEP

By J. L. HODSON
("Press and Journal" War Correspondent)
WITH THE BRITISH ARMY IN FRANCE,
Friday.

TO-DAY, along with other war correspondents, I accompanied Lord Gort, C.-in-C., on a visit to an Army Corps headquarters and afterwards to one of our crack Highland regiments who are busy five or six hours a day digging a reserve line of trenches several miles behind the Front.

It was a dry winter's day, with steely sun and biting winds.

Most of us were muffled up and feeling the chill, but Lord Gort wore neither greatcoat nor gloves. He didn't seem to notice the cold at all.

He is fifty-three years old, but he strode about in the soft brown clay that nearly sucked your boots off, and jumped into and climbed out of seven feet trenches, like a young man.

He looks as tough as the Scots who were digging those trenches, and that's saying a lot.

This was the first time I had set eyes on him. I nearly fell over him at Corps Headquarters, where I opened the door not knowing he was on the other side! He didn't growl, but just said "Good morning."

He is stocky and broad, with grey eyes rather sunken, beetling brows, the closest clipped sandy moustache I ever saw, and his hat worn rather far back and a little on one side. He walks with a hustling gait as though ready to shoulder any one out of the way.

QUERY TO MEN

I expected to see him in immaculate field boots, but he just wore breeches and puttees like any junior infantry officer.

As soon as he had inspected the Highlanders' guard, which presented arms, he asked every man in it where he came from.

[...] question he [...] a score of times or [...] round the old barn [...] a hole [...] straw, which at one [...] feet high, the Scots [...] lives comfortable.

[...] one blanket and a [...] it they said they were [...] were full of fun. When [...] I asked them how [...]

And: "No [...]"

London-Scottish at Inverness, 1939

Aberdeen Football club players, Strauss, Armstrong and Cowie, enlist for the Royal Corps of Signals at the Music Hall

THE SECRET WAR

THE BIG HOUSE

The daily news bulletins during World War Two did not report on events going on behind closed doors – events which were to play an important part in the final outcome of the conflict. For instance there was no mention of a country house in Inverness-shire which helped to win the war.

Deep in the Highlands lies a house which is fast becoming a crumbling ruin, taking with it secrets of disembowelling, sabotage and political assassination.

These were just some of the activities on the curriculum at Inverailort House, which established a reputation as the leading paramilitary "finishing" school for secret agents in occupied Europe.

Nowadays it would hardly merit a second glance from tourists travelling through the picturesque Inverness-shire countryside, but sixty or more years ago it was a strategically important centre for one of Sir Winston Churchill's war-winning enterprises.

The decaying mansion lies just off the road between Fort William and Mallaig.

The Big House, as it was called in its heyday, became the British centre for "ungentlemanly warfare" from the summer of 1940 until the end of World War II.

Winston Churchill, who had remarked that Hitler didn't play cricket, set up the Special Operations Executive (SOE) to develop all forms of irregular warfare which would ignore the accepted rules of engagement.

Under the guidance of Sir Colin Gubbins, a Scottish officer who had first-hand experience of the guerrilla methods used by IRA controller Michael Collins in Ireland, the SOE launched a network of training centres across rural Scotland.

The legendary Lord Lovat, who trained and led the secret-service commandos on D-Day, requisitioned the house from its reluctant owner and set up the centre of special training.

Major Henry Hall, who today lives at Aboyne, recalls his time there and the men responsible for the specialised training.

"It was a typically military set-up, but the training was very specialised," he said.

"It was focused on subterfuge, which meant anything from one-on-one fighting with a view to killing to blowing up trains and other strategic targets."

Fake sabotage attempts on the main line to Mallaig would prepare the agents for actions against Nazi targets in occupied Europe.

"I remember that well," said Major Hall.

Men of the Royal Engineers march down Union Street on their way to the station on October 9, 1939

"We used to have to put charges on the line and appear to blow up the train. The train drivers actually became quite used to it and would often lean out of the train after an explosion and give us a thumbs-up, saying 'That was a good one'.

"I dread to think what the passengers who were not regular travellers on the line might have thought, but I should think there were a few who might have believed that Scotland was under attack."

It was a tough course. The Russians believed that it took 10 years to fully train a special agent, but at Inverailort, the course was an intensive 10 weeks.

There were other training centres in the area at Traigh, Meoble and Arisaig, and each centre had its own nationality assigned. There were Czech freedom fighters, French resistance members and others from various parts of occupied Europe.

Special agents from the SOE's Scottish centres carried out numerous daring operations behind enemy lines, including: the destruction of a Norwegian dam which was central to the Nazis' research into the atom bomb; the assassination of the fascist protector of Bohemia; and the sabotage of transport links in France on the eve of the Normandy landings.

While Sir Colin Gubbins was the principal of the centre, there were two unlikely instructors in William E. Fairbairn and Eric Anthony "Bill" Sykes. The two men could easily have passed for bank clerks nearing retirement age, but they were experienced fighting men and still very capable. In one introductory display to the new recruits, they both fell down a full flight of stairs, landing at the bottom in combat position with a gun in one hand and knife in the other.

William E. Fairbairn had been assistant commissioner of the Shanghai Municipal Police (SMP). He and his colleague, Eric Anthony Sykes, had needed an effective system to teach their officers so that they could survive the harsh realities of the roughest seaport in the world. In all the training that Fairbairn set for the SMP in his role of chief instructor in self-defence – arrest and restraint, shooting, disarming, house raids, bodyguard work and riot-control techniques – he strove for a sense of realism. His men were pressure tested in all they did.

"They showed us all kinds of things," said Major Hall.

"Their whole ethos was get it over with quickly and get on with the next task. They completely ignored the Geneva Convention. It was what was needed at the time. Churchill had pointed out that Hitler did not play by the rules and therefore he needed people who would be able to handle the same ruthless way of fighting.

"Fairbairn was the first European to win a black belt in judo and he had written a book called *All In Fighting*. Sykes looked like an amiable clergyman, but he was equally as tough and frightening as his colleague. They were the sort of men who you were glad were on your side. They overlooked nothing. We even had a gentleman loaned to us from Peterhead jail to teach us how to blow safes."

The 5/7th Gordon Highlanders are put through their paces in camp

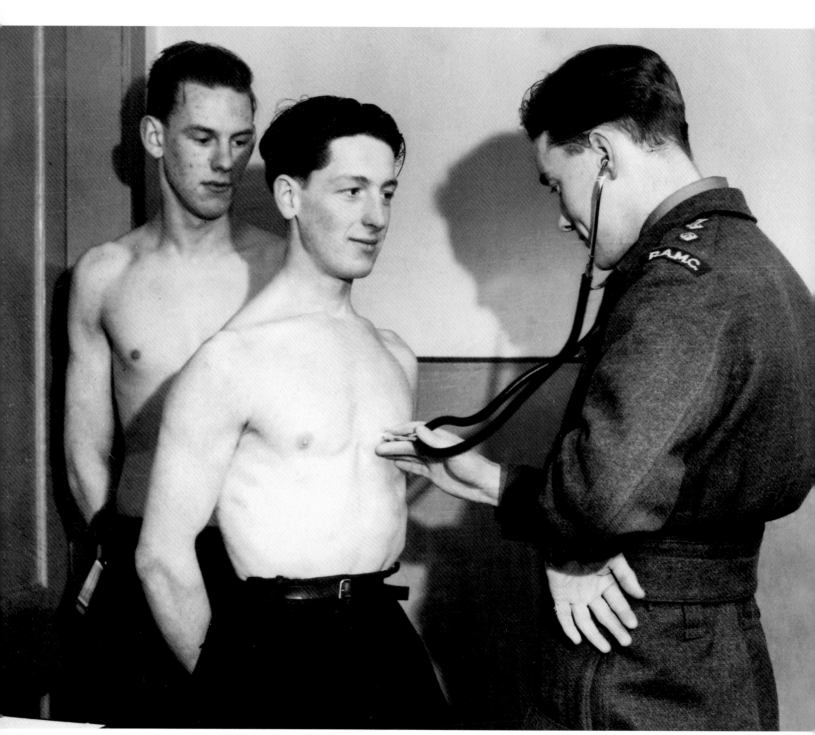

Medical examination of conscripts at Bridge of Don

Following the cessation of hostilities, Fairbairn, the inventor of the commando knife, went to Canada to train agents for OSS, the forerunner of the CIA.

Among the men who trained at Inverailort were actor David Niven and Kim Philby, later to be revealed as a Communist spy.

"Among other things, you were also taught how to live under a regime that you hated," said Major Hall.

"If we were in a situation in which we were to spend some time as an ordinary member of the public in a land governed by the very regime we were opposed to, we had to give nothing away, so that was part of the training course, too."

Kim Philby obviously learned a great deal.

Members of the SOE played a major part in the final victory, but at no time were their activities publicised, even after a success. They remained covert throughout the war, and in some cases, to this day.

After the war, Clement Attlee became Prime Minister and one of his first decisions was to disband the Special Operations Executive. It was the formal end of the secret army created by Churchill.

Inverailort House can still be seen, now in a state of decay, but a close look reveals that there was far more to the place than simply a family home. There are clear signs of its contribution to the war effort, but many of its secrets will remain with it forever.

RAMC Nurses at
Cruden Bay, 1940

ON THE CONVOYS

The Arctic convoys which took military supplies to the Soviet Union during World War Two were characterised by great courage and endurance by all who served in them, among whom were Torry man Eddie Bewick who especially recalled the hazards of being at sea in northern waters during the night.

"We were aboard an anti-aircraft ship which was converted from a Fyffes banana boat. The biggest problem was that it was bright daylight at midnight so we were always easy to find," he said.

The convoys had to run the gauntlet of almost continual attack from German bombers and U-boats based in occupied Norway. But that was not all for there were ferocious winter gales, perpetual darkness during the winter and constant daylight in the summer as Eddie Bewick noted.

The convoys were assembled in Loch Ewe in Wester Ross and also in Iceland. A typical convoy was PQ18 which sailed with its escort from the loch on September 2, 1942 commanded by an Aberdeen man. It was destined to become the most heavily attacked convoy of the war.

The previous convoy was the tragic PQ17 which scattered under orders and lost 24 of its 37 merchant and rescue ships at the hands of U-boats and attacking aircraft.

Further Russian convoys were delayed because of the need to transfer forces to the Mediterranean for the relief of Malta. By the end of August the convoy could go because the necessary ships had returned from their mission.

Rear Admiral Robert Burnett was appointed to command the convoy's close escort. Born in Old Deer he belonged to a well-known Aberdeenshire family, the Burnetts of Kemnay. He had joined the Royal Navy at the age of 16 and served during the First World War. Burnett was a tough, no-nonsense tactician and had the essential qualities of strong leadership and physical endurance as well as great experience. It was fitting that he flew his flag on the new anti-aircraft cruiser HMS *Scylla* because she was Aberdeen's adopted warship. During Warship Week in 1942, Aberdonians raised £3.5 million to pay for the ship.

Among the escort's destroyers was another of Aberdeenshire's adopted warships, HMS *Somali*.

PQ18's close escort was the heaviest ever given at that time to a convoy and consisted of *Scylla*, 29 destroyers, the escort carrier HMS *Avenger*, five armed trawlers and two rescue ships. The *Avenger* carried six Hurricane fighters and three Swordfish anti-submarine aircraft. This was, of course, pitifully small compared with the might of the Luftwaffe but Burnett was confident the fighters would be able to break up attacking formations.

In Loch Ewe the merchantmen assembled laden with tanks, vehicles, aircraft, explosives, fuel and other war supplies for Stalin's Red Army. There were British, American, Russian and Panamanian ships including the US's *Patrick Henry* which was the first of 2,770 Liberty ships built in US shipyards to replace those sunk by the enemy.

The convoy sailed first to Iceland where other ships joined it. On September 13, off Spitzbergen in the Barents Sea, the fiercest convoy battle of the war began with U-boats sinking two merchant ships. Later, 44 Heinkel He 111 torpedo-bombers attacked like 'a huge flight of nightmare locusts'.

Avenger failed to get her Hurricanes airborne in time and, despite the intense hail of anti-aircraft fire, the Heinkels pressed home their attack and released their torpedoes at point-blank range. They sank eight ships for the loss of only five aircraft.

The next day the US ammunition ship *Mary Luckenbach* was hit and disintegrated completely. Debris from her showered down on the neighbouring ships like hail. Amazingly there was one survivor, a young black steward who had been walking along the deck carrying a cup for coffee for the master when the explosion blew him clear of the wreckage.

Aboard the *Scylla* was Reuters correspondent Arthur Oakeshott who wrote a vivid description of the battle. As the torpedoes sped towards the cruiser, he wrote, "The brilliant

Gordon Highlanders route march and feeding time in camp

seamanship of the skipper turned the ship with the rapidity of a motorist swerving a car. The 'tin-fish' swished harmlessly past our stern." *Scylla's* gun-crews acquired an expertise in gunnery which earned her the nickname the 'Toothless Terror' - toothless because of the apparent small calibre of her guns for a light cruiser but terror for her accuracy and amazing rate of fire.

The convoy steamed on leaving behind in its wake a trail of debris floating in the Arctic Ocean. The air attacks persisted, although none was as ferocious as the first.

So far, the convoy had paid dearly with 13 ships lost. Rear Admiral Burnettt considered whether to go on and risk further losses or to return home with what was left. He went to his Bible for inspiration and opened it indiscriminately at Isaiah chapter 43 and read: "When thou passest through the waters, I will be with thee and through the rivers, they shall not overflow thee. When thou walkest through the fire, thou shalt not be burned, neither shall the flame kindle upon thee. For I am the Lord thy God."

Burnett finished reading and went to the chart-room where he told his staff officer, "We carry on and we'll not lose another ship." He was proved right and there were no further losses.

By September 17, the ships' crews were almost at the point of exhaustion with 21 hours our of 24 on duty. On *Scylla*, Oakeshott observed that her crew spent most of their time at action stations. They never had their clothes off for upwards of 14 days and washing and shaving was a rarity because of the need to conserve water.

The convoy finally reached the port of Archangel on September 21. Burnett's fighting destroyer escort had proved its worth by providing a protective screen around the convoy. In reply the escorts and Avenger's Hurricanes had shot down about 40 German air raft and destroyers had sunk two U-boats.

Burnett's achievements had helped wipe out the stain of the PQ17 disaster.

Perhaps it was best summed up by an American survivor who told Oakeshotte, "You talk snooty but you're great guys and your destroyers are swell."

A company of Gordon Highlanders march through Kintore in 1938

VILLAGE SECRET

A tiny Angus hamlet played its part in turning the tide of World War Two when it hosted a high-powered Russian delegation on their way to change the course of history.

The key role of Tealing in the signing of the crucial Anglo–Soviet Treaty in 1942 – a pivotal point in World War Two when the Nazi blitzkrieg raged against Russia – was only uncovered some 60 years later.

The treaty, which paved the way for the Allied victory, was signed by Stalin's foreign minister, Vyacheslav Molotov, who made an undercover trip to the United Kingdom to meet Winston Churchill at Chequers.

Few details of the secret visit have emerged, as a complete news blackout was imposed for two weeks after Mr Molotov's arrival, but it has long been believed that the foreign minister made his way to London by train.

However, local researcher Sandra Burke discovered that Mr Molotov flew to the village aerodrome in a TB7 Russian bomber on the first leg of his mission. The Russian minister was accompanied by 16 Soviet officials when the bomber thundered on to the runway at Tealing, now the site of a chicken broiler plant.

Witnesses in the village recall that the distinctive Russian bomber flew low over the northern part of Dundee on the morning of May 20, 1942.

One local WAAF sergeant who worked at the aerodrome recalled, "Britain didn't have anything like it at the time and we were all stunned by the sheer size and presence of it.

"There was little pomp and circumstance – the priority was to ensure that Mr Molotov's arrival and departure went smoothly."

The Soviet delegation was taken from Tealing, five miles north of Dundee, in Minerva limousines hired from a local firm and driven to Errol aerodrome 12 miles away.

On arrival at Errol, Mr Molotov was given the choice of two aircraft for London.

The aircraft Mr Molotov did not choose crashed in the Vale of York, killing members of his staff and RAF personnel. Mr Molotov himself arrived safely for the signing on May 26.

Dr Paul Vysny, of St Andrews University, said, "Stalin was really the guy in charge and Molotov was a very faithful henchman.

"If Molotov had chosen the plane that crashed and hadn't signed the treaty, it would have complicated relations between the Soviets and Britain. The treaty was very important in ensuring co-operation between the UK and the Russians against Nazi Germany and, of course, it was very contentious because of the situation of Poland.

"Britain ostensibly went to war to defend Poland, and the Russians had been fighting with Germany against Britain under the terms of the Nazi–Soviet pact.

"But needs must, and in the circumstances of World War Two, Britain had little choice."

Gordon Highlanders route march through Ellon, 1938

Gordon Highlanders route march through Banchory, 1938

MONTY'S BODYGUARD

Old soldier Alan Glennie could write a book about his astonishing wartime adventures. At 81 Alan is able to recall every grim – and sometimes comical – chapter of his war career.

He recalls proudly how the raw country loon became batman and then bodyguard to World War Two legend Field Marshall Montgomery.

The retired Aberdeen record store owner – who supplied the Queen with her favourite hits on vinyl – also remembers standing to attention "in awe" of US General Eisenhower.

The son of a Tarves farmer, Alan went from being a hairdresser to crack army sniper to record shop owner.

Among his collection of wartime medals is an Africa Star – decorated with one bar.

Alan was one of seven men appointed to protect Montgomery.

"He was a bit of an acid drop really, but he gave us whisky," said Alan. "He was teetotal and used to get car loads of whisky.

"He was a nice person but a very difficult man. He didn't speak very much to us – it was a case of 'yes sir, no sir, three bags full sir'.

Alan was just 19 when he was called up.

"It was my baptism of fire," he said. "I was a very raw recruit with the 5th-7th battalion of the Gordon Highlanders and I was sent to El Alamein.

"I remember going in to action for the first time. It was midnight and we were marched into the desert, five foot between each soldier. It was just a walk through hell – the tracer bullets were knee high. It was terrifying."

But Alan's sniping skills led to the rank of lance corporal and, ultimately, batman to Monty.

As Monty's batman, Alan never left the General's side. As a result, he met Eisenhower in Germany.

"He was very austere," said Alan. "We always got pep talks but we hardly spoke to him. I just held him in awe."

Alan was in Germany when war was declared over.

"We were crossing the Rhine in wee boats when the Red Caps told us the news," he explained. "It was such a relief."

HUGH WAS NO COWARD

Hugh Fraser was one of nearly 200 soldiers who refused to leave their own regiments and join the battle for Salerno in southern Italy in 1943.

Believed to be too scared to pick up their arms and fight, they were branded cowards.

The mutineers were found guilty, stripped of their campaign medals and sent to prison camps.

Soon after the war ended, a report cleared them of cowardice. It found their prime motive was excessive loyalty to their own units.

But the damage had been done and many of the mutineers were deeply psychologically scarred and died young.

However, Hugh carved out a successful career as a policeman.

Hugh later explained, "We refused to obey orders because we had been deceived and lied to by our officers. All we wanted to do was fight with our own regiments."

In 1942 the young Queen's Own Cameron Highlander was shipped to Egypt to fight in the North African desert campaign against Rommel.

Struck down by infected desert sores in the summer of 1943, he was transferred to a hospital in Tripoli.

There he joined around 200 wounded and exhausted soldiers who had been among the heroes of the victory at El Alamein.

All were desperate to rejoin their comrades and carry on the fight against Hitler.

Officers confirmed they were being shipped back to their own divisions.

However, halfway through the voyage, they were suddenly told they were all to reinforce the 46th and 56th divisions at the battle for Salerno.

Hugh said, "We were speechless. Shocked. Angry.

"It was blatant deceit. Deliberate lies."

When the ship docked in the south of Italy, the soldiers were ordered to join the 46th on the Salerno battlefield. A few marched but another 191 did not move, despite being warned the sentence for mutiny was death.

The mutineers – all from the 51st Highlanders and 50th Tyne Tees – were frogmarched to a cage next to a compound of German prisoners of war.

A few days later they were shipped to a military prison in North Africa and faced a mass court martial.

All were found guilty of mutiny. Three sergeants were sentenced to death. Hugh, a corporal, was sentenced to 10 years in prison.

However Field Marshall Montgomery, who needed every man for the push through Europe, ordered their immediate release.

After fighting in the battle for Anzio, Hugh was machine-gunned in the chest and ended the war as a clerk at the Allies' Italian GHQ.

In the late 1940s, he joined Aberdeen City Police and joked about being the only mutineer in the force.

Gordon Highlanders route march through Banchory, 1938

Bomb damage on Menzies Road in Torry, Aberdeen Tenants salvaging undamaged property

HERO ON AND OFF THE PITCH

Wartime football usually meant players guested for clubs depending on where they were stationed but, for former Aberdeen forward Archie Baird, it meant surviving prisoner of war camps.

A former pupil of Rutherglen Academy, Glaswegian Baird played junior football for Strathclyde alongside Willie Waddell, who went on to have a distinguished career with Rangers.

By 1938, Baird's performances in his six months in junior football had attracted attention from all over Britain.

Blackpool, Swindon Town, Partick Thistle and Motherwell all made approaches for the tall striker.

None, however, convinced Baird's mother she should allow her son to sign for them.

Baird recalled, "David Halliday came down from Aberdeen to speak to my family. I was being chased by a few clubs, but David met with my mother and she was in no doubt he was the man I should sign for.

"I always remember my mum telling me he had honest eyes and that was the reason I should sign for Aberdeen, so I did what I was told.

"I'd always admired Aberdeen's style of play and I looked upon moving to Aberdeen as an adventure. My signing-on fee was £20 and I was paid a weekly wage of £4."

But the outbreak of World War Two meant the young Baird was to be denied his chance to play for the first team – for the time being at least.

He said, "I didn't get the chance to play as I was sent to France with the Royal Army Medical Corps in 1939 when I was 20.

"During the war, you guested for other clubs depending on where you were stationed and I made a couple of appearances for Leeds United and Aldershot when I was in England.

"We were moved about so often, so I didn't play that much."

The lack of football was disappointing for the young Baird, but his duty for his country had to come first.

Serving in the armed forces, however, proved to be a harrowing experience as Baird was captured by the Germans in 1942.

"I was in the North African desert while on duty with the British Expeditionary Force and we were forced back towards Mersa Matruh on the border of Egypt. I was with the field ambulance and we were out with an infantry patrol when we were surrounded by a squadron of German tanks and taken to El Adem, near Tobruk.

"We were moved around several POW camps, but the conditions were not pleasant to say the least. I was 6ft 2in and I dropped from 12st to eight due to malaria and dysentery.

"The sanitary and hygiene were very poor and many prisoners became ill.

"Even when we were prisoners, football was one of the things which kept us going and I played for Scotland against Wales in one of the camps."

Archie was eventually moved to Rimini in Italy, where conditions were much better. Red Cross food parcels were delivered and Baird's health improved considerably as a result.

By September 1943, the chance to make a break for freedom arose and Baird grabbed it with both hands.

"Eventually, Mussolini and Italy pulled out and the Germans moved in. The Italians just deserted the camp and we had to decide whether to make a run for it or stay and wait for the Germans to arrive.

"Needless to say, I didn't think long and hard about it. I made a break for it under the wire fence along with a Geordie fellow called Harold Smith."

Escaping from a POW camp was one thing, but getting out of Italy was a far more difficult task. The duo found refuge with an Italian family and earned their keep on the farm, working in fields, sowing and ploughing, and helping to make wine.

"I was behind enemy lines for nine months, but I found shelter with the Pilotti family.

"When I was living with the family, I started learning Italian, as I had to if I was to survive."

The Allied troops may have been winning the war, but the resulting chaos almost cost Archie his life.

"When the war was coming to an end, the Germans were retreating towards where I was staying.

"I was walking along the road, carrying a sack of grain with some Italians, one of whom was slightly drunk and laughing a lot.

"We met a German patrol on the main road and one of the soldiers took exception to the hilarity, believing the young Italian was laughing at him.

"He pushed the Italian over and pulled out his gun, declaring, 'In the name of the Fatherland, I should shoot you'.

"He asked me why I was not in the army and was very suspicious of me as he had never come across a 6ft 2in Italian before.

"Thankfully, my Italian was better than his and I managed to convince him I was looking after my widowed mother and the youngster was not mocking him, he was merely drunk.

"He warned the young lad not to insult him again and left us on the side of the road, and it proved to be a real let-off for both of us."

Eventually, the Germans retreated out of Italy completely and Baird was a free man again.

This one is just a practice but there was the real thing still to come

THE PRESS AND JOURNAL, Monday, May 13, 1946

DONS' TRIUMPHAL TOUR AFTER HISTORIC WIN

Nation-Wide Congratulations On Popular Victory

From Our Own Representative

WHILE Aberdeen awaits impatiently an opportunity to greet the eleven men who made football history on Saturday by defeating Rangers 3-2 in the League Cup final and bringing the first national trophy to the city, Glasgow and the West of Scotland acclaimed them on Saturday night.

Crowds stood cheering loudly in the streets of Glasgow as the bus, gaily bedecked with red and white ribbons—the team's colours—took the Dons from the scene of their great triumph at Hampden Park to the North British Hotel.

There were cheers again as the team and officials left the hotel after dinner to return to their quarters at Largs.

The journey from Glasgow to Largs was a triumphal tour with people gathering in the streets of the towns and villages through which the bus passed to cheer the victory-flushed Dons.

Messages of congratulation by telegram and telephone reached Largs from all parts of Scotland on Saturday night.

Outstanding figures in Scottish football hailed Aberdeen's victory, representatives of teams defeated by the Dons on their way to the final sent their "Well done" messages, and from Aberdeen and the North-east came hundreds of expressions of pride and joy.

"Doubting Thomas"

Mr Thomas Loudon, stationmaster at the Joint Station, the man who saw the Dons' supporters at Hampden safely off from Aberdeen in the special trains, was doubtful about the result.

In a telegram sent to Mr William Mitchell, chairman of the Aberdeen club, he said—"Heartiest congratulations. A doubting Thomas repents, I am very happy."

Sir Thomas Mitchell, the Lord Provost, who attended the match, voiced the citizens' congratulations in the Dons' dressing room after the final.

The 16,000 spectators from Aberdeen and the North-east who went to Glasgow by road, rail and air joined in one of the most amusing scenes of enthusiasm seen in the famous Hampden enclosure.

They kept up a continuous roar of applause for ten minutes during the cup presentation ceremony.

Hopes and Ambitions

Receiving the cup from Provost D. A. Gray, Airdrie, president of the Scottish Football Association, Mr Mitchell spoke of the North's hopes and ambitions of victory, and his happiness when they were realised.

The climax in this scene of enthusiasm came when Willie Cooper, the Dons' captain, with the cup, to the cheering thousands, was carried shoulder-high from the field by his team-mates, with Johnstone and Lord Provost to advance to enter.

The winning goal, fifteen seconds from time, which won the Scottish League Cup for Aberdeen at Hampden on Saturday. Shaw, the Rangers goalkeeper, is seen spreadeagled while "Tiger" Shaw and Young of Rangers look on disconsolate. ("The Press and Journal" copyright.)

Finally returning to Scotland in 1945, the war had undoubtedly changed him, but he was determined to resurrect his football career at Pittodrie and set about resuming where he had left off seven years earlier.

Baird's return proved to be an enjoyable one. One of his most memorable moments came on May 11, 1946, in the Scottish League Cup final against Rangers at Hampden in front of 135,000 spectators. Baird scored the opening goal after just 90 seconds in the 3–2 win for the Dons.

Two other finals in less than a year made for an exciting return to Scottish football.

Baird recalled, "We got to the final again in 1947, but were beaten 4–0 by Rangers. But we did make the Scottish Cup final that year, beating Hibs 2–1.

"The memories I have of all three finals are the same. We played to more than 100,000 people at each final, with 135,000 watching us win the League Cup in 1946.

"I scored in the first minute when Stan Williams flicked on a long throw from Andy Cowie and I headed the ball in.

"I remember a sea of people greeting us at Joint Station – something ridiculous like 15,000 people – and we were treated like returning heroes."

To complete his rehabilitation, he was also capped by Scotland, playing against Belgium in 1946.

But the years in captivity took their toll on Baird and injuries were becoming a regular occurrence. Three cartilage operations and a hairline fracture of his left tibula disrupted his career and he moved on from Pittodrie in 1953 after 144 appearances and 37 goals.

BRITAIN AT WAR
DID YOU KNOW?

UNDERGROUND stations became hostels during the air raids and at the peak of the bombing some 177,000 were sheltering every night on the platforms.

LUX Toilet Soap did their bit for the war effort by issuing an information leaflet on how to get the most usage from a bar of soap. For one ration coupon a 3oz bar of Lux soap could be bought for threepence halfpenny. No wonder it had to last!

STOCKINGS were in short supply and some girls took to colouring their legs with gravy browning. It might have made their legs tasty but looked very strange if they were caught out in the rain!

TULIPS did not come from Amsterdam much during the latter part of the war. There was such a food shortage during the winter of 1944–45 that the Dutch started to roast their tulip bulbs for a food which was eatable but likely to cause indigestion.

THE BLACK MARKET on mainland Europe was often infiltrated by the Gestapo. This was not so much to keep tabs on what was going on as to supplement the incomes of the officers involved. One of the prime merchandise was potatoes which were supplied by northern European countries to those of the south. Wine went in the other direction and cigarettes were as good as Euro currency.

LONDON TRANSPORT lost so many red buses during the air raids that it called in country buses to keep the capital moving.

ROMFORD might not sound the place for making history but on June 5, 1942, it witnessed a first that would change the face of British shopping for ever. The Co-operative Society of Romford launched Britain's first self-service grocery store.

WOMEN were forced into part-time work in May 1943 as part of the re-organisation of the nation's workforce. All working women between the ages of 18 and 45 saw their jobs compulsorily become part-time.

Three men in charge of all those women! Munitions factory workers freeze history

PEOPLE AT WAR

MY STORY – WALLACE McINTOSH

Wallace McIntosh was for a time the most decorated air gunner in the Royal Air Force but that only tells a fraction of his story, a tale which would grace any Hollywood movie screen.

"I was born in Logierieve, near Udny, although we later moved to Perthshire," said Wallace. "We were a farming family and I was the eldest of 11 children.

"I never thought as I was growing up that I would do anything but farming, but I suspect that very few people knew how their life would change course so rapidly because of another world war.

"I had little formal education so when I joined the RAF as war was breaking out I became a general duties airman.

"I was not much use to them for anything that required academic knowledge. I did regret that.

"I had never considered my lack of real education to be important before but it came home to me that it could stand in the way of any progress I wanted to make."

Wallace was nothing if not determined and made up for his lost schooling by working hard at studies that would serve him well in the RAF. His new-found knowledge and his obvious dedication earned him promotion.

"My promotion meant that I could really get into some action and I was trained as a gunner.

"It was a far cry from the kind of life I had expected back home on the farm and I was very excited when I climbed into the gun turret of a Lancaster bomber for the first time."

Little did Wallace know that in the years ahead he would fly more than 600 hours with the RAF and play a major part in the success of Operation Overlord.

"Once I had climbed into the Lancaster for the first time, I seemed to be on duty non-stop for the next 18 months or so. For D-Day the 207 Lancaster Squadron was on round-the-clock sorties. We had been briefed only hours before although we were well aware that something very big was about to happen. Morale was high in the RAF even though there were regular losses of men and machines.

"Our first duty was to bomb areas of France, softening up the big guns at La Pirnelle on the Cherbourg peninsula. Our mission lasted for four hours and we were quite tired when we returned, although any fatigue soon vanished when we were sent out again on a night flight over the invasion beaches." The skies were far from clear of the enemy and Wallace and his comrades were soon under attack.

"I spotted a Junkers 88 coming in to have a go at us," said Wallace. "I warned our pilot and he went into combat manoeuvre. We then opened fire and hit the enemy aircraft pretty hard. It immediately started spinning towards the ground with flames coming from both its engines.

"Almost immediately another Junkers 88 came in to attack. I think we had got our eye in by now because we hit the plane with another burst and it just exploded in front of us and the pieces started to plunge towards the ground.

"We were pretty keyed up after that and it seemed like only a few minutes, although it was really about half an hour, when another enemy aircraft flew at us to attack. This one was an ME210. Once again we hit it with a burst of fire and went into a dive. We watched as it plunged towards the sea and saw it burst into flames just before it splashed into the water."

Three enemy planes shot down in little more than half an hour was a remarkable achievement.

"You never really thought about it that much," he said. "You were aware that you had done the job and there was a sense of elation that you had won that particular conflict but other than that it was all very matter of fact.

"I can remember one of our senior pilots, a wing commander, joking over the intercom as we were on our way home through particularly heavy flak that he was going to put the wheels down and roll home on it."

That particular kind of humour kept morale high. The survival rate for Lancaster bombing crews on those dark days over Europe was only about one in five but Wallace never doubted that he would be a survivor.

"It never crossed my mind that I would ever be shot down or taken prisoner," he said. "Certainly there was fear. The first time we were hit by flak was a frightening experience. It made you realise that you were not impregnable. Somehow you got used to it though."

The report of the events on D-Day were cited when Flying Officer Wallace McIntosh was awarded his Distinguished Flying Cross which he received from King George VI at Buckingham Palace.

"That was a very proud day for me of course and I shall never forget it but it is the experience of D-Day itself which I most remember," said Wallace who still has his flying logbook as a souvenir.

Remarkably his only comment alongside the log of the D-Day action was "Quiet trip?"

"I didn't really know what else to say," he revealed. "Compared to a lot of people, it was a quiet trip. We came back in one piece."

That "quiet trip" earned Wallace a personal telegram of commendation from the legendary Air Marshall "Bomber" Harris, head of Bomber Command.

"That was a nice and unexpected gesture from a great man," said Wallace. "I am proud of the DFC and the DFM which I received but we were there to do a job. I know that might sound a bit of a cliché but that is how we felt about it."

Wallace's logbook swelled to more than 600 flying hours and 55 operational sorties. He knew Germany from the air so well that he hardly needed navigation and could recognise every major German city from 2000ft.

His personal tally of eight enemy aircraft served to make him one of the most celebrated members of 207 Squadron, their very own "top gun".

Wallace later returned to Scotland and Dyce where he now lives and in Civvy Street he became a senior executive with an agricultural supplies company, his peace–time occupation closely related to his early farming life.

Few people who met him in his business role would have realised that they were shaking hands with a man who was the "Braveheart of the Skies".

Aberdeen's Music Hall decorated for Salute the Soldier Week, May 1944

MY STORY – ALF CHEETHAM

Life has been quite an adventure for Aberdeen's Alfred Cheetham. His 20 years as a tea planter in West Bengal and Assam, India, contained more experiences than most people live through during their years but probably his military service during the war even outdoes his tales from Asia.

Alf Cheetham volunteered for active service shortly after the outbreak of war.

"I wanted to do my bit although I was in an apprenticeship which absolved me from conscription. My father had arranged the apprenticeship, not to keep me out of the war but to help me with a career."

Alf's most vivid memory is of D-Day when he was serving with the 3rd Recce and found himself in the thick of the Normandy fighting.

"I need not have been there on D-Day because I could have taken that apprenticeship but I would not have missed it for all the world.

"The 3rd Recce was a new and special services regiment, created for speedy attacks," said Alf.

"The regiment had been converted from the 8th Northumberland Fusiliers and every man had to pass the most stringent test.

"We wore brown berets with leather brims and our colours were green and yellow. Our badge was forked lightning with a spear signifying our motto of 'Spear of the attack and as quick as lightning'.

"As well as the extensive training in combat and endurance, every man also had to be able to drive a vehicle wheeled or tracked as well as being an assault trooper. We were formed for a special task and when the war ended the regiment was disbanded, job done."

"We had very little notice that we were going in for D-Day. Our training meant that we were constantly on red alert and ready to go anywhere, anytime, so there was no real need for us to have lengthy preparations. We were never told what we were going into until the last minute.

"We invaded Sword Beach and fought our way inland to join up with the 6th Airborne troops who had landed by parachute to take the Pegasus Bridge over the Caen Canal.

"The landing itself was quite an experience. We had waterproofed our armoured cars for just such a event and had to disembark into about 6ft of sea water. As we left the vessel we sank straight into the water and it seemed to be an age before we came up again and were able to drive.

"Having fought our way through we parked our armoured cars in an orchard and set off on foot. I became isolated and when a grenade exploded nearby I landed in a ditch. My leg had been hit by shrapnel and I was quite badly wounded. The next thing I knew I was being pulled out by German soldiers. In an instant I had become a prisoner of war.

Bread is sold in the streets in the aftermath of a raid

"I must admit to having been out-soldiered and allowed myself to be cut off. I didn't know what had happened to the others. I was then taken with some other prisoners to a railway and we were crowded into filthy cattle trucks and taken across France and into Germany to a new 'offlag' at a place called Falkenhaugh."

Alf had not undergone extensive training for nothing and he kept a keen eye on any escape opportunity.

"One day we were marshalling in one of the open yards at the camp and myself and a chap from the 6th Airborne saw our opportunity," Alf recalled. "I forgot about my leg wound and just took off.

"Amazingly we got away with it and ended up at a place then called Plan.

"Some nuns took me in and cared for my wound. They looked after me until the American forces caught up with us and eventually I was flown back to Britain in a Dakota and found myself being cared for in the Princess Royal Mental Hospital. I don't think there was anything wrong with my mind but in those days anywhere that resembled a hospital was put to use to care for the war wounded."

Later Alf was put in charge of vehicle maintenance training at Catterick but when the war was over he went to Aberdeen University before embarking upon a civilian career which took him to India as a tea planter.

Many years later, Alf and his headmistress wife, Clare, went on holiday to France and visited the famous Pegasus cafe which was the first house to be liberated in France on D-Day.

"It brought back a lot of memories to be in the area once again," said Alf. "My wife could speak French and she explained to Mme Gondre, the proprietor and the lady who, with her late husband, had lived in the house when it was liberated, that I had been among those soldiers there on D-Day.

"The place just erupted and I was treated like royalty. Everyone was buying me drinks and I have never had so much brandy in my life. How I managed to drive us to Le Havre later on I have no idea. It came home to me just how much being liberated meant to those lovely people.

"However, while in conversation with Mme Gondre, she told me that I really should visit Ranville Cemetery. Ranville is the nearby village, the first to be freed during D-Day.

"I went along and there I found some of my old friends, comrades of the 3rd Recce who had fallen, some of them obviously struck down during that same attack which had wounded me.

The Press and Journal

ABERDEEN, FRIDAY, JUNE 9, 1944   THREE HALFPENCE

EVERY GERMAN ASSAULT FLUNG BACK

Our Caen-Bayeux Line Firmly Held

VON RUNDSTEDT has now deployed his reserves and thrown them into action along with the whole of the front in Normandy. Very heavy fighting is taking place inland, it was learned at Shaef early this morning.

But British and American troops continue to make progress on all fronts and the Allied bridgehead is gradually being developed.

No great advances have been made, but at no front have we been driven back.

The line is firm in the Caen-Bayeux region. Fighting continues on the lateral road running east from St. Mere Eglise (half-way between Carentan and Valoches).

"It was a poignant moment to stand there in the silence. In my mind I could see their faces and hear their voices, their nervous laughter. They were brave men and I felt a great sense of honour and privilege to be standing among their graves."

For Alf Cheetham, World War Two was an adventure that he wishes had never been necessary but since it did happen he is glad to have taken part and even more glad to have been able to go back and salute his old comrades of the 3rd Recce A squadron.

*An ARP exercise,
December 1939.
Cleaning Department
workers have sand for
extinguishing
incendiaries and water
and masks for
decontamination*

*A shortage of men for
these dances. Stay at
home holidays, July 1944*

German POWs
in the North-East
in 1946

POWs working on the roads – believed to be in the Seaton Park area

Hon. Peter Fraser, Prime Minister of New Zealand, visits Tain and Fearn, 1941

*Monty during a brief
visit to Aberdeen,
accompanied by
Colonel McKenchnie
on his way to lunch at
Bridge of Don barracks*

Clement Attlee visits a lumber camp at Glenmuick, 1942

MY STORY – BILL LOGIE

In a ceremony at the French Embassy earlier in 2005, former bombardier Bill Logie joined some of the most famous people in history by receiving the Légion d'honneur. It is the highest tribute France can pay for gallantry in action or for distinguished service in military or civilian life.

As a teenager brought up in Woodside, Aberdeen, Bill found himself in the teeth of some of the most bloody action of World War Two. Bill was a member of the Royal Artillery and he was responsible for radar tracking to pinpoint mortars and other Nazi targets as the Allies pushed across Europe.

One of his darkest hours was when his boat, the *Malayan Prince*, was lying off Caen while being bombarded by Allied aircraft. "An awful lot of lads were killed by friendly fire. But we didn't talk about that," said Bill. "It was not as rare an event as we would like but that is the sort of thing that can happen during a war."

Bill landed and was just outside Caen when someone said it was July 13.

"I suddenly stopped and thought, 'That's my 21st birthday.' And that was that. Celebrations? Don't be ridiculous!"

Over the past decade the former clerk has organised regular pilgrimages by veterans back to the killing fields but the award of the Légion d'honneur was something extra special.

The grandfather-of-two said at the time, "This is a great honour. When I receive it I will think of the thousands of young men who gave their lives for their country."

It was established by Napoleon in 1802 and Sir Winston Churchill is one of the most famous of those to receive the French honour.

A former pupil of Woodside Primary, Hilton Secondary and Robert Gordon's College, Bill became a clerk with the Caledonian Milling Company in Palmerston Road when he left school.

He was called up in 1942, aged 18, and sent to the 60th regiment Royal Artillery.

Bill was demobbed in 1947 and joined Shell Mex in Aberdeen's Albyn Place.

A year later, he married Margaret and in 1951 they moved to Huntly. They had a son, Derek, and daughter, Elizabeth.

Derek died of a stroke in 1990 and Margaret died five years later.

Bill retired from his job as a wholesale shoe distributor in Huntly in 1988 and in typical modesty nobody was more surprised than he when he learned of the Légion d'honneur award.

"I was very surprised, thrilled of course, but very surprised," he said. "It was a very great honour and thoroughly undeserved although I am very proud of it. In truth though I think everyone would swap their medals and memories for the chance to turn back the clock and make sure that it never really happened."

LORD LOVAT

Legends are created during times of strife and they do not emerge much more legendary than Lord Lovat.

Lord Lovat had already earned quite a reputation for courage even before his famous D-Day heroics. He believed in leading from the front and never asked his men to do something he would not do himself.

His D-Day exploits have been immortalised on film but even before the momentous day dawned he was awarded the DSO and promoted to brigadier. He was a physically powerful man at 6ft but more than that he was a powerful man in personality and everyone who served under him agreed that they had implicit faith in his leadership.

Simon Christopher Joseph Fraser, Lord Lovat, was a man with Hollywood looks, a strong presence but a gentle and humorous approach to everyday life.

His family heritage was intertwined with Scottish history for centuries and he graced the family name well. His family seat was Beaufort Castle, Beauly. Lovat was a politician as well as a military man but also as a laird he was held both in esteem and affection by all his staff and tenants.

His father had formed the original Lovat's Scouts for the South African wars by shaping a unit out of his gillies and deer stalkers. Our Lord Lovat continued that and when he was placed in charge of a commando unit there were many volunteers to join him although only a comparatively few stayed the full training course. Lovat himself had learned much about endurance and field fighting tactics on training exercises as far away as Arizona.

He was not only a great trainer of men but was passionately interested in various forms of sport and had trained race horses as well as fighting cocks. He took a great interest in the physical preparation and psychological approach to both competition and warfare.

His training of commandos was a legend all of its own. He took them to the Highlands with live ammunition and taught them speed, decisiveness and initiative, sometimes telling them that they would have an early morning rendezvous the next day 50, 60 or even 80 miles away. Where it was and how they were to get there was up to them to discover.

In the great D-Day plan, Lord Lovat and his men were told that they would be needed to support the 6th Airborne Division. When briefed by the general in charge, he was told, "Yours will be the first help we shall get. You will be landing on the beaches 10 miles away and you will have to fight your way across country and I want you there on time. You land on the beaches some time after 8am and I want you to be at the bridges for 12.15. Do you think you can do it?"

Lovat's reply was, "We may be a bit pressed now and then, sir, but at 12.15 we will be there. We won't let your paratroops down."

Lovat led his men through enemy fire which was fiercer than expected and at 12.14 the

Airborne Division had just about given up hope of seeing them when suddenly through the smoke and noise they heard the skirl of pipes.

Lord Lovat's own piper, Bill Millin, led the way to the astonishment of the enemy and Lovat himself followed behind with rifle over shoulder and pistol in hand. Behind them came a long line of green beret commandos.

They crossed Pegasus Bridge under fire and Lovat had his hand heartily shaken by a brigadier of the 6th Airborne Division.

Lovat grinned, looked at his watch and simply said, "I'm sorry we are two and a half minutes late."

In the film, *The Longest Day*, he was played by Peter Lawford but even that drama did not match up to the real-life legend. His war time exploits continued despite being wounded at Normandy and later he was awarded the Légion d'honneur and the Croix de Guerre by General de Gaulle.

The citation paid tribute to his training, support and counsel of the French commandos as well as the deeds of himself and his own troops during the war and in particular on D-Day.

He was hailed as "an incomparable leader in battle" and that is exactly how he has been remembered – a hero of the 20th century, and more especially, a hero of D-Day.

Women train as motor mechanics at a Government Emergency Training Centre, November 1942

MY STORY – DON MASON

RAMC Nurses at Cruden Bay Hotel, 1940

Aircraft hummed across the darkened sky on the night of June 5 as the D-Day invasion got under way. On board a Stirling Troop Transporter was a flight crew of six men and among them was wireless operator Don Mason who is now 83 and lives in Thurso. He clearly recalls the tension of that night flight to victory.

"I was in the Coastal and Bomber Command when war broke out, but from 1941 I joined 620 Squadron 3 Group Bomber Command until December 1943, when life began to change," said Don.

"We began to suspect that something was being planned when the squadron was transferred to 38 Group Airborne Support and our Mark III Short Stirling four-engine bombers were replaced by a Mark IV version of the same aircraft which had a parachute exit in the floor of the fuselage and a glider towing attachment beneath the rear gun turret.

"The aircraft still had its bombing capability and with the extra dropping possibilities, we were to be engaged in SAS and SOE operations dropping supplies to resistance movements in occupied Europe. The bomb bays would carry containers rather than conventional bombs."

It was not quite that simple though as the then WO Mason discovered. "During the first half of 1944 we suddenly started training with paratroops and glider formation towing," he explained. "This was a departure from what we had been doing so we were starting to get a little excited.

The youth organisations did their bit. Here come the Boys' Brigade to collect salvage

"That heightened when in May of that year it was noticeable that security around our base at Fairford was stepped up considerably. Boundary fences were repaired and strengthened and service police with dogs appeared. Obviously something serious was definitely afoot.

"During the latter part of May the base was closed up completely. No leave was allowed and everyone was confined to camp. Mail was censored."

Don and his comrades knew that they had to remain patient before being told what was going to happen but they also knew they would not have to wait for long.

"Paratroops from 6th Airborne began to arrive and tents and field kitchens were set up on the airfield while we continued our airborne training. Finally, on June 4, we were ordered to a briefing for Operation Tonga, part of the Overlord plan to invade Europe. We finally learned what all these preparations were about.

"It was impressed upon us that our navigation and timing had to be perfect in order to achieve the objectives set, namely to deliver the paratroops to an exact location at a precise time, namely the Ranville dropping zone at 01.10 hours."

Don said that later they were told the whole operation was postponed for 24 hours due to weather problems, so they had some time on their hands to reflect on what was to come.

Finally, late on June 5, it was time to make a start and the paratroopers were loaded into the planes.

"We also took Guy Byham, a BBC war correspondent, and we were ready and eager to get going at the appointed time of 23.10 hours," said Don. "It was a quiet night with little cloud and the moon above. You could feel the tension.

"As we left the south coast and flew across the Needles on the Isle of Wight, we began to see hoards of shipping of all sorts and sizes and as we approached our mid-channel turning point we came across a melee of craft at what appeared to be a staging point. I believe it was a holding and gathering station for shipping, code-named Piccadilly Circus.

"We were about three minutes early at this point and had to orbit to get back on time, a dangerous manoeuvre across a stream of aircraft but a necessary one since we had to be time perfect. As we approached the Normandy coast we noted some light flak and tracer and descended to our drop height of 800ft.

"It was my job to leave my post at the radio, move to the rear of the fuselage, lower a strop guard to prevent the parachutists' static lines from fouling the tail plane elevators of the aircraft and to open the exit door in the floor of the fuselage.

"The red light appeared, troops stood up, shackled up their static lines and when the light changed to green away they went with lots of raucous yelling. At this point a Dakota aircraft flying just ahead and above us released its stick of troops and we flew right through them, miraculously not hitting one of them. I bet it gave them a scare seeing four great props hurtling towards them.

"All this time there were bangs and bumps from flak burst which did no harm except for pieces of shrapnel rattling on the metal skin of the plane.

"It all sounds very calm, almost droll to describe it all now but it was a highly tense and exciting flight."

That was not the end of the show for Don Mason and his comrades. In the afternoon of June 6 they were briefed for Operation Mallard.

"We had to tow a Horsa glider loaded with an armoured jeep, four anti-tank guns and

The Duchess of Gloucester on an official visit to an Aberdeen munitions factory in 1942

their crews. They were destined for the same Ranville dropping zone that we had visited during the night.

"Daylight gave us a very different view of the beaches which where clogged with vehicles, landing craft, debris, smoke and explosions. The hornets' nest had been well and truly stirred. We encountered much more flak on this flight and we were something of a sitting target since we were at 1200ft and flying at a maximum of 135 knots while towing. A glider could not be towed at a greater speed because it would break up.

"We could not take any evasive action either so we just had to run the gauntlet.

"All 16 of our squadron's aircraft were damaged and one was brought down on the beachhead. We lost four aircraft and three crews in those operations on D-Day. As for me, I went on to take part in many other operations including five to Arnhem, scene of one of the bloodiest of battles and the subject of *A Bridge Too Far*.

"Sacrifice is always demanded by war and we should never forget the fallen or fail to honour their memory. Anyone who was there will tell you that D-Day still lives on within them."

Don Mason's story typifies the great role played by the RAF during the conflict and once again vividly illustrates the importance of the co-operation between the various forces.

TEENAGER AT WAR

Rita Hadden was only 14 when Scotland and the rest of Britain was dragged into World War Two. In a *Press & Journal* interview she vividly recalled the way it was for her and youngsters like her.

The build-up to World War Two after Germany invaded Poland passed young Rita Hadden of Aberdeen by as she explained.

"We were only 14 and weren't politically minded," she said. "But I do remember September 3, 1939 very clearly."

"I had just left the school that July so I was working at Broadford's mill and I stayed in Froghall Avenue with my parents and my brother and sister.

"I remember it was a Sunday and we knew the Prime Minister was going to make an announcement.

"At 14 you weren't that interested in news, but that day we all gathered with our ears to the wireless. Everyone was silent. There wasn't a movement in the street – and it was a big street.

"Then Chamberlain came on and said we were at war with Germany. Everyone was just shocked and stunned. I ran in next door to my chum's and we just stood there. I never liked Chamberlain after that.

"We didn't know what to expect, how long it was going to last, what would happen to your chums but we were 14 and didn't worry too much about it.

Survivors of the attack at Wellington Road, Aberdeen

"Then the boys were drafted out, huge processions of them marching to the railway station and in came gas masks and rationing. You didn't know what to make of it."

While Glasgow received the worst damage of Scottish cities from enemy bombers, Aberdeen was actually on the receiving end of most attacks north of the border. Enemy aircraft returning from sorties on the central belt to Germany and Norway would empty any leftover bombs over the north-east, regularly wiping out houses, farmland and the fishing fleet.

Throughout the war, torpedoed, mined and bombed ships regularly limped in to north-east harbours while Fraserburgh and Peterhead were devastated by attacks from the air and mines washed in by the tide.

Despite this, the government urged people to think positively through the heavily censored press which banned photographs of devastation in Britain.

One of the messages makes for bizarre reading, stereotyping the stiff upper lip British resolve: "Don't Lose Your Head – in other words, keep smiling. There's nothing to be gained by going about with the corners of your mouth turned down and it has a bad effect on people whose nerves are not so good as yours. So, even if a bomb falls in your street – which is unlikely – keep smiling."

While Aberdeen was on the receiving end of many relatively small air attacks, nearly 100 people were killed during a devastating raid on the city on April 21, 1943.

Shortly after 9pm, as dusk fell, 25 German aircraft each carrying over two tons of bombs hit many areas in the city, including Woodside, Hilton, Kittybrewster and George Street.

The raid killed 98 people, seriously injured 93 and struck 8,000 homes.

By this time, Rita was 17 and tired of false alarms from the air-raid sirens.

"I was at the City Cinema in George Street with my chum and we went to a place on Hutcheon Street for a pie and peas," she said. "The sirens had gone off but being young and daft and thinking about boys we just stayed where we were.

"The next thing, the bombs fell and we all dived out of the place. We went to a lane and waited for the all clear.

"On the walk back to Froghall you could see nothing but fires, fallen buildings and glass all over the place.

"When we got to Froghall there wasn't a window in the area that still had glass in it. We were lucky because the bombs didn't land on Froghall and we just got the blast.

"There was a big crater in Fraser Place and two blocks of houses in Elmbank Terrace were just all on the ground.

"Some families have never been found to this day. It was terrible. During the war, everyone helped out. Whenever anyone got sad news everyone rallied round and supported them. It was hard for an awful lot of families when the telegram boy arrived. You always feared the worst."

Throughout the war, Rita consoled many friends who lost family in the conflict.

Just after the war, she married Robert Meres who served in the Merchant Navy and grew up alongside her in Froghall.

They have two children, three grandchildren and one great-grandchild.

"Many, many people died in the war," said Rita. "Too many."

Her story is typical of youngsters growing up during the conflict and trying to keep some sort of normality in her life as the world went insane.

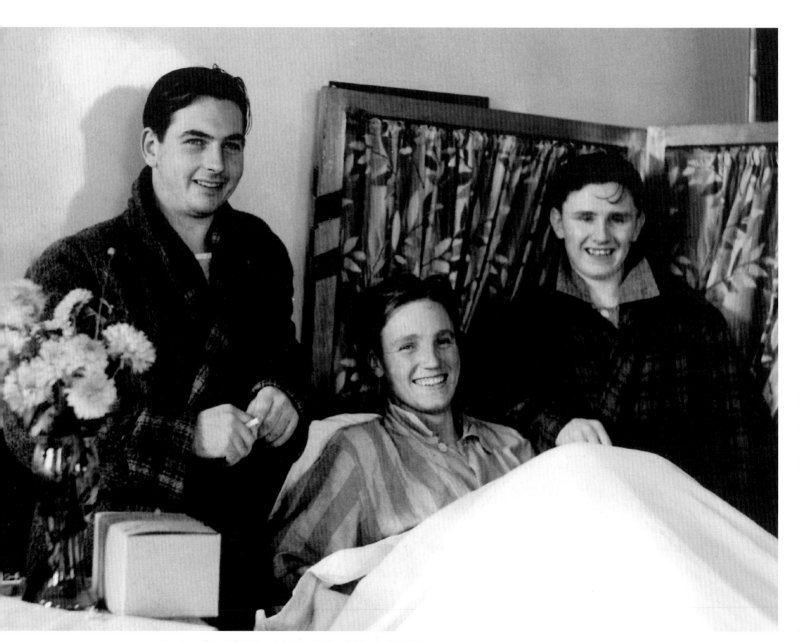

Survivors from HMS Royal Oak in Kirkwall Hospital, 1939

Bomb damage to
Aberdeen Beach
Promenade, July 1, 1940

Earl De La Warr,
Chairman of The Flax
Board, visits the flax
factory at Turriff, 1942

The aftermath of the April 21st raid. The funeral cortege for Bedford Road and Cattofield victims winds its way down Seaforth Road en route to Trinity Cemetery

MY STORY – ERIC JOHNSTON

Eric Johnston had a promising career in banking when World War Two interrupted the life of millions like him. From the serenity of the bank he found himself amid the noise and destruction of battle and vividly recalls his time as a member of a Sherman tank crew.

"I was still at school, a bursary boy at Aberdeen Grammar, when war broke out but we were on half-day schooling and I got a part-time job in a bank, really as a career beginning," said Eric. "When I left school I went full-time of course and the bank manager was in charge of the local Home Guard division."

If that sounds familiar, Eric describes himself as the Private Pike of the unit.

"It was very much as portrayed in *Dad's Army*. I can certainly see many of the characters in our unit corresponding to those in *Dad's Army*, including myself as the youngest whose mother kept an eye on what he was doing and made sure he did not go out without his scarf.

"I spent much of my time doing guard duty at Aberdeen gas and electricity works. My boss was a former World War One army officer and I learned quite a bit about army life in a short time from him."

When he was old enough, Eric joined the Royal Armoured Corps as a volunteer.

"I was just 18 when I went along to the recruitment office in Woburn Hill. I had wanted to join the RAF but I was turned down because my sight was not absolutely perfect.

"The next best thing seemed to be the tanks and since I was a volunteer I could choose which regiment I could join.

"At the recruitment centre I met Major John Cripps whom I learned was the brother of Stafford Cripps, then Chancellor of the Exchequer. He didn't say much to me except to tell me to take my hands out of my pockets."

For the next six months Eric and his fellow 18-year-old recruits underwent intensive training in driving, maintenance, gunnery and wireless with tank crew members having to be interchangeable.

"When we passed out we were given the choice of regiment and I joined the 4/7 Dragoon Guards. In 1943 we learned that we would be one of the regiments which would lead the invasion of Europe with a secret weapon, an amphibious tank.

"We were later introduced to the vehicle which was a DD (Duplex Drive) Sherman tank fitted with twin propellers and an inflatable canvas screen to give buoyancy. The plan was to launch the tanks from Tank Landing Craft (TLC) at 5,000 yards offshore to arrive on the beach just before the infantry.

"Our training took us to Fort George in January and after a very wild night at sea aboard the TLC it was decided the sea was too rough to launch the tanks so instead we had to wade them ashore in Burghead Bay.

"It was an interesting experience and my first encounter with something that was to visit me quite often in the times ahead, sea sickness. It affected all of us. The wade ashore was quite pleasant by comparison."

After gunnery practice at Tain, Eric and his comrades were sent to the south coast for more landing training at Studland Bay.

"We lost six tanks and six crew in one exercise because the sea was so rough. Even D-Day itself was put back 24 hours from June 5 because of bad weather," said Eric.

"When the big day came we were apprehensive of course but there was no time for actual fear. The sea was rough again and most of us were seasick once more. I think that helped in a funny sort of way because we could not wait to get ashore.

"We were due to land on Gold Beach at 'H-Hour minus 5" which was 7.20am with the infantry landing at 7.25. However, the unexpected happened and the sea remained too rough for the tanks to be launched from a distance and the TLCs had to take them in for a deep wade to the beach.

"On the beach to our right, Omaha, the Americans launched 32 tanks and 27 went down with their crews.

"This made a huge difference to fire support to the infantry on the beach, contributing to the high American casualties at Omaha. In the film, *Saving Private Ryan*, Tom Hanks shouts, 'There are no DD tanks on the beach.' That was an authentic line.

"The 4/7 Dragoon Guards lost five tanks either 'drowned' or mined on the beach. More were lost later in the day when a navy spotter thought they were enemy tanks and the ship opened fire.

"It was not unusual for 'friendly fire' to destroy our own tanks and men but it was considered to be an occupational hazard in those days.

"There was no time for self-pity or fear as you were working hard all the time. Each tank crew had to do its own cooking, dig its own trenches for sleeping and really work independently while under orders. You were focused on what you were doing but you were aware of the noise and the mayhem that was going on around you. It was almost impossible to tell how it was all going other than how you were doing yourself.

"Most of us only reflected for a few minutes before grabbing whatever sleep was available. I think I reflect far more now on the events of that day than I ever did at the time."

The days that followed saw fierce fighting as the Germans brought up their tanks in a tough defence.

"A third of our tank commanders were killed or wounded in the first 10 days," said Eric.

"I was with the regiment throughout the battles that followed. I continued writing home to my mother once a week just to let her know I was still in one piece. We were not allowed to actually give any details of where we were or what had been happening.

"I'll never forget June 17 because it was Derby Day and we could listen to the race commentary on the radio. We couldn't believe that the Derby was being run while all this was going on but we listened anyway.

"I got knocked out during a fracas that day and lost all my possessions. We were not encouraged to carry much so there was nothing really personal."

Finally it was all over.

"It ended for us in Bremerhaven in May 1945 when we were attached to the 51st Highland Division and took part in their victory parade on VE Day. I was one of the lucky ones because I had lost three tanks in all but only suffered minor injuries.

"We were not allowed to keep diaries but I used to scribble a few notes now and then. I have never really needed those notes because D-Day is all still so vivid in my mind. I can still hear the noise of engines, of both small arms and artillery fire, of shouting, fear and pain.

Land Army girls on parade in 1941 "It was a job that had to be done and how grateful we were to have survived, although we could not help but shed a tear for those who had fallen."

LOVE AT FIRST SIGHT

EVEN after more than 60 years, Belle Connell still gets emotional when she remembers that first meeting with her husband-to-be.

It was 1943 and World War Two was raging.

Fred was a dashing, 19-year-old flying officer at RAF Lossiemouth, where he was training as a rear gunner for bombing missions over Germany.

Belle, from Inverness, was a corporal in the WAFS at the same base, doing the vital work of packing parachutes and dinghies.

Belle says, "It was the height of the war and we knew Fred was going to be on dangerous missions. Like so many other couples in those days, we knew we had to be sensible and not become too involved.

"We knew we mustn't become too serious about each other because we would soon be separated and probably never see each other again.

"I knew only too well how dangerous being a rear gunner was.

"The chances of Fred being killed were high. Many of his comrades never came back from their mission."

Sure enough, Fred was soon posted to another base in England from where he carried out 34 missions over Germany in Halifax and Lancaster bombers.

During the action he once had to bail out when another bomber crashed into his.

And he was responsible for shooting down two Luftwaffe fighters as well as two daring missions during the D-Day landings.

The young airman's bravery was eventually rewarded with the Distinguished Flying Medal.

More than a year later, when the war was all-but won, Fred was posted back to RAF Lossiemouth – where he again came face-to-face with 19-year-old Belle. On January 6, 1945, the couple were married at Elgin registry office and later made their home in Inverness, where Fred became an officer at Porterfield Prison.

The Connells went on to have David, now 58, Bryan, 57 and 55-year-old Freda and in 2005 they celebrated their diamond wedding anniversary

It was a war-time romance that went right and has stood the course of time. So what has been the secret of a happy marriage for the couple who met in battle-torn Britain?

Fred says, simply, "It was love at first sight and we have loved each other ever since."

A beautiful baby competition in July 1944

MY STORY – JIM DUFFUS

General Montgomery stood in a dusty square in Sicily in October 1943 and addressed the troops standing before him. Among those troops was Aberdeen's Jim Duffus. For him that address was the start of D-Day

Jim Duffus stood in that square in Sicily along with other members of the 51st Highland Division and listened carefully to the words of the man they knew as their great war leader.

"You are going home," said Montgomery, "not to parade about with your medals but to take part in future operations in Europe."

It was a profound statement – the seeds of D-Day had already been planted.

"We read between the lines," said Jim, "and we guessed that no matter how things were looking, the tide was about to turn. All of us there had taken part in the invasion of Sicily and we realised that we were looking ahead to the prospects of even more intensive activity.

"We put that to the back of our minds though as we landed back in dear old Blighty on a cold November in 1943. We were greeted by messages on walls which simply said, 'Second Front Now!'

"We had a glorious six months in the UK, rejoicing in being on home territory but also undergoing further training in preparation for the future operations in Europe which Montgomery had mentioned."

Jim Duffus was born and bred in Aberdeen and was an apprentice motor mechanic while also serving in the Territorial Army.

He joined up and was into action almost immediately but D-Day was to be the highlight of his army career, a day which he recalls vividly.

"June 6, 1944 saw us on a transport ship approaching the coast of France with the navy blasting away with their big guns," said Jim. "Looking over the rail of the ship we saw the assault landing craft coming alongside and we were soon clambering down the rope net ladder with full kit and weapons.

"There was a swell on the water which made the landing craft rise and fall about six feet. The sailors on board shouted to jump when the deck was going down. We would

Newfoundland umberjacks, nverness-shire, 1940

Queen Elizabeth visits the naval hospital at Kingseat in March 1940, accompanied by Lord Provost Mitchell

have risked a broken limb with our heavy kit if we had jumped as the deck was rising."

At last it was time to head for the beach and Jim and his comrades prepared to fling themselves into the fray.

"Heading for the beach the American navy commander announced that he would not go too far in as the tide was starting to go out and he did not want to get stuck and become a target. So the ramp went down and we clambered off in about four to five feet of water. The swell was lifting men off their feet with their heavy packs and tending to make them lose their balance.

"The soldier 'queuing up' behind me was a little chap and he urgently told me that he couldn't swim. I tried to reassure him and helped him down into the water which was very cold. He kept a tight grip on my arm while I quietly talked to him until we reached the beach with the sea streaming off our kit. It was not until later that I realised that in trying to reassure him I had actually helped myself to stay calm."

Immediately Jim and the others reached the beach they were into the action. "That beach had been taken a short time before by Canadians and these sons of Canada were lying where they had fallen.

Demolition of the antitank defences on Aberdeen promenade, April 1946

"We followed a white tape through a minefield up the sand dunes, passing the remains of a Royal Engineer who had been clearing the mines.

"We were all a lot happier when our boots hit the hard road and we quickly formed up into sections and started marching.

"Our trousers were soaking wet and we were chafing in places 'where the sun don't shine' but we kept going at a fair pace while, in true British army style, we were cursing everyone from Eisenhower down!

"As we passed a field hospital with a row of bodies outside and the screams of the wounded coming from inside we fell silent. As darkness fell we bedded down in a long ditch at the edge of a field.

"I faced what I thought was the direction of Aberdeen and silently toasted my mother and father who had thoughtfully put a half gill of Glendronach malt whisky in my kit on my last leave."

The next morning there was a rude awakening as a German fighter plane flew over, machine gunning the field.

"It woke us up pretty quickly and we then moved to support our comrades of the 6th Airborne Division at Benouville, better known as Pegasus Bridge," said Jim.

"My battery commander, Major David Kirk, from Glasgow, and his driver Gunner Frank McClure, from Arbroath, were killed by a 'Moaning Minnie', a multi-barreled mortar, at 1st Gordons HQ, a few days later.

"About an hour before he was killed Major Kirk jokingly said to me, 'There's no future up here Duffus!' The two men lie together in Ranville Cemetery. I have visited their graves on the 40th and 50th anniversaries and, God willing, will do so again this year.

"Frank McClure was always singing 'You Are My Sunshine' and after his death we never sang that one again at any battery singsong."

The memories for Jim Duffus never fade. Like others who have survived to this day, their experiences live on in the sights and sounds of their minds.

"I have comrades lying at El Alamein, Tripoli, Sicily, France, Holland and Germany and I still think of them all.

"If I may, I should like to dedicate these memories to the laughing young faces of the lads who never got the chance to grow old."

The young Princess Elizabeth inspects Sea Rangers at the opening of the Sailors' Home, Aberdeen

MY STORY – ERNEST ROBERTSON

Fighting on the beaches would never have been possible but for the outstanding work of the Royal Navy. Able Seaman Ernest Robertson saw action on board a destroyer

Ernest Robertson thought that he and his shipmates were going to miss playing a part in D-Day when he watched the landing craft leaving base but then came the order, "Hands to stations!"

Ernest was a young lorry driver before he volunteered for the forces.

"I was 18 at the time and I enlisted here in Aberdeen and received the King's shilling. My welcome from the Petty Officer was, 'You'd better hurry up and catch the train or you'll be in trouble on your first day.'

Bomb damage at 55 Wellington Road, Aberdeen

"A bunch of us left Aberdeen to go to Devonport. We were all leaving our families and friends so there was an instant comradeship which I think we were all glad of because homesickness was a problem long before we tackled any seasickness."

After his initial training, Ernest joined HMS *Montrose*, a destroyer with the task of escorting Russian convoy supply ships.

"We saw a little action but it was fairly quiet although very cold at times," said Ernest. "It was always a pleasure to return to British waters even though there were still hazards.

"We were based in Harwich at Parkstone Quay and were in base for a few days with other destroyers when one by one the others left their moorings and were replaced by landing craft. It did strike me as being odd and it was obvious that something was up but I did not really take any more notice than that.

"Our task at the time was to paint various parts of the ship and we were pretty busy because we never knew when we were going to put to sea again."

Late on June 5, 1944, the landing craft began to move.

"They were flying both the stars and stripes and the white ensign and there was something about the way they set off which caused quite a buzz among those who witnessed it. We guessed that something serious was under way and that could only mean one thing.

"I think we all felt a bit left out, if this was going to be as big as we thought, we didn't want to miss it. Suddenly as the last of the landing ships had cleared the harbour we received the call, 'Hands to stations for leaving harbour!' The mood changed immediately and we were soon on our way to join the others."

Once again HMS *Montrose* was called into escort duty.

"We were protecting the troop carriers and I believe we were actually escorting the 7th Armoured Division. Our course took us round and close to the south coast until we reached the Isle of Wight. We then turned south and steamed quite slowly across the channel in what was a very wide and busy road of traffic.

"There were ships of all sizes and descriptions, American and British, and the sky, although dark, was clearly full of aircraft. There were masses of them, especially bombers, and I couldn't help thinking that Germany or wherever else they were going was going to get the pounding of its life. I never saw one German plane just British and American. It was an unforgettable sight."

As HMS Montrose neared the French coast it was apparent that a major battle was under way. "You could hear the gunfire and smell the cordite fumes long before we saw the French coastline," he said. "It was clear that this was a massive push. As we got closer we began to see what was happening and there was a huge battle in progress. Other troops were already engaged before ours were close enough to the beach to join in.

"The three beaches which involved British troops were Sword, Juno and Gold. I think our lot went into Gold. We were told to get as close in as possible and we did just that."

Their job complete, the crew of HMS *Montrose* dropped anchor that evening just clear of the beach.

"It was about 9pm so it had been a long day," Ernest recalled. "We were tired and allowed to rest a little although we were on full alert the whole time. There was a little time to reflect on how it had gone so far. From our point of view, it had gone like clockwork.

"It was difficult to tell how things were going on land but we got the impression that, despite many casualties, it was going as had been hoped and that meant that the possibility of the war ending was becoming all the more a realistic hope."

The following morning HMS *Montrose* was on the move once again.

"We had to escort the troop ships back to Britain. It was almost a relaxing journey. Knowing that the troop carriers were not needed for the immediate future was very encouraging because it meant that they were making progress and did not need a possible escape route."

As we know, it was another ingredient in the success of D-Day and a great debt is owed to sailors like Ernest Robertson and the Royal Navy.

"It was an extremely exciting day and one which I shall always remember throughout my life," he said. "I am proud to have been a part of D-Day and very glad that it all went so well."

Ernest still lives in Aberdeen and vividly recalls the events before, during and after D-Day.

"I don't think I could ever forget it," he said. "Every detail is vivid in my mind. After all, it was one of the most important military successes in history. I am proud to have been a part of it."

Facility visit at Alastrean house, Tarland in 1943. Lady MacRobert is on the right of the picture (pointing)

HORSEBACK TO SPITFIRE

As a rookie soldier Fergus Davidson trained for the cavalry, fighting on horseback with a sabre at his side. But by the end of World War Two, he was piloting one of the most sophisticated and legendary instruments of warfare, the Spitfire.

In 1939 Fergus joined the cavalry – but had dreamed of flying since he was a boy.

As soon as the chance came he transferred to the RAF and was posted to Tangmere, already famous for its role in the Battle of Britain.

Fergus flew numerous night-fighter missions from Tangmere before being transferred again. This time it was reconnaissance duty over the English Channel.

In 1943 Fergus joined a Supermarine Spitfire squadron based in Malta where he helped defend the island from Italian and German forces.

He said, "Malta was very difficult during the war. Some of the locals were using caves as makeshift bomb shelters and a lot of them weren't too happy about us being there. They thought it wasn't their fight and some let us know that."

Nothing will detract from the first time Fergus flew a Spitfire, a memory that has stuck with him.

He said, "I remember coming off the runway in Malta. There were no thermals, the air was still and the Spitfire just cut through the air like a vampire in flight."

But, after many aerial escapades, Fergus was brought crashing to earth, forced to bail out over enemy territory.

He suffered rough treatment at the hands of his Italian captors before being handed over to the Germans, questioned by the Gestapo and finally holed up in POW camp Stalag Luft 6.

Near the end of the war the treatment of prisoners worsened. Fergus recalls being loaded into cattle trucks to be moved.

He said, "It is quite incredible how many people you can fit in a carriage at bayonet point.

"I couldn't even move my hand down to my pocket to reach a potato I had hidden."

Just after being shot down Fergus was invited to meet the German pilot responsible.

"He was just a bit older than me and didn't speak much English. But you could tell by the look in his eye we had flying in common.

"The Germans didn't see us as their enemy. They did not want to be fighting us.

"He gave me his chocolate ration and I said, 'Maybe some day we will fly together.'"

"We actually saw the blokes we were battling with. It was a personal thing but you never forgot that we were at war."

King George and Queen Elizabeth in Aberdeen, March 10 1941

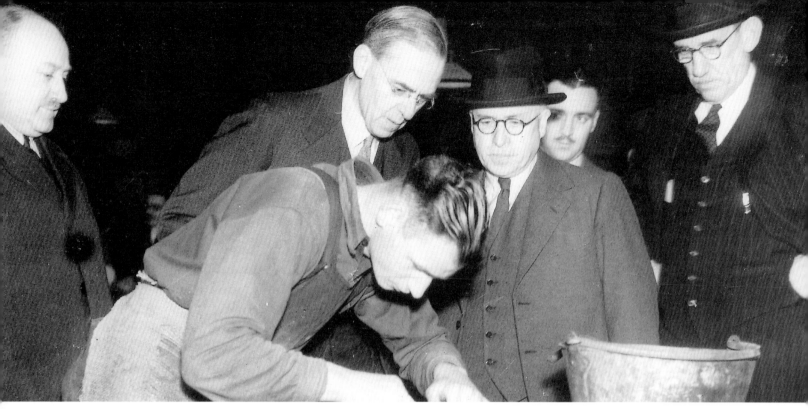

Sir Stafford Cripps tours a Fraserburgh factory

MY STORY – ALEX BROWN

Around 5am on D-Day, Alex Brown was on an American Liberty ship along with hundreds of other troops sailing out of Tilbury.

He said, "While we were waiting to embark, a dispatch rider went past and I heard him say to someone, 'The invasion has started'.

"We all just wanted to get on with it."

When the first lorries drove off the ship on to Gold Beach, they sank beneath the waves.

Alex and the rest of the drivers were ordered to wait until the tide went out before attempting the landing.

Alex's tough, D-Day battle took the form of relentless days and nights of firing and, being under fire, manhandling huge boxes of ammunition for the gunners.

Gradually, they pushed ahead – and the Germans further back – into France.

"We dug trenches for cover.

"Shells whistled constantly overhead and mortars exploded around us.

"We had 16 big guns which fired day and night. Boy, those gunners were exposed but they were a crack team.

"Sometimes the Germans were only 2000 yards ahead of us. We could even hear them speaking and arguing.

"Those of us who had been in the war for years got to the point where all the shelling didn't bother us.

"But it was tough on some of the younger ones just out from home.

"There was one young lad of 20 who'd recently got married.

"Back in Britain, his new wife had said to me, 'Please, look after my husband for me.'

"He was in a bad way every time there was a boom or explosion. I asked the doctor to see he got back to the beach. He couldn't take much more."

Eventually, the German lines were broken and British troops began chasing the enemy through France.

Alex was among the proud soldiers who fought and won the battle to free St Valery from the Germans. Hundreds of Gordon Highlanders had been captured there four years before. They had finally been avenged.

Alex remembers the delighted, cheering civilians as he marched through Belgium and Holland.

One of Alex's most haunting memories of his five years' service in World War Two came one sweltering afternoon in the North African desert.

It was 1942, shortly before the historic battle of El Alamein.

Alex was a 22-year-old driver in the Royal Army Service Corps.

"I was driving a jeep across the desert this red-hot afternoon – 300 yards between each vehicle, as ordered.

"Suddenly this bird the size of a pigeon swooped low towards my jeep.

"It started circling silently round and round me.

"It gave me a strange, eerie feeling.

"A feeling that no matter what happened in the war, I was going to be OK.

"As if the bird was somehow protecting me.

"I thought about that a lot during some of the most dangerous times.

"And sure enough, I never got hit."

Alex saw action right across Europe and North Africa.

After leaving Rosemount School in Aberdeen at 14, Alex took a succession of jobs, including delivering the Co-op milk with a horse and cart.

Alex's younger brother, Robert, served with the Scots Guards. Sadly, he died in Aberdeen Royal Infirmary of peritonitis, aged just 25.

Alex joined the RASC the day after his 22nd birthday, at the beginning of 1940.

Six months later, the young rookie was on his way to northern France.

Alex served in the ammunition unit, spending much of his time with explosives strapped to his back.

However, the Germans had the British Expeditionary Force beaten and Alex was one of the thousands who retreated to the beaches of Dunkirk.

He waited for three days for a boat before finally being picked up and shipped back home.

By 1941, Alex was in Egypt, then fought in the historic battle of El Alamein as part of the famous the Highland Division.

Part of his job was night missions up ahead of the front. He laid ammunition for the infantry and artillery to collect as they pushed forward.

He also buried tons of land mines.

"The most vivid thing I remember about Alamein is that one minute there was total stillness in the desert and the next, the deafening explosion of our 800 guns."

Alex and his fellow Scots pushed forward – sleeping by night and fighting by day – until they reached Algiers.

Then south, to the invasion of Sicily.

After that his division was posted back to Britain – to prepare for D-day.

"It was top secret, but I had a fair idea of what was going on," chuckles Alex.

"I'd been working in the officers' mess and, because they were totally unaware of me, I heard some things I shouldn't have.

"Then they must have realised, because the adjutant had me in and read the Official Secrets Act to me.

"He told me not to say a word about what I'd heard. Or else, when all the rest of the guys were going home, I'd be staying here."

Alex's war ended in May 1945 when his sergeant broke the news, "It's finished."

"Everyone started shouting. It was an overwhelming sense of relief. We knew we were going home.

"That night, we lit a bonfire."

Gas mask distribution for adults

A Wellington aircraft crashed on landing at Dyce on May 16 1945, wrecking a goods train in Dyce railway station. Two airmen were killed

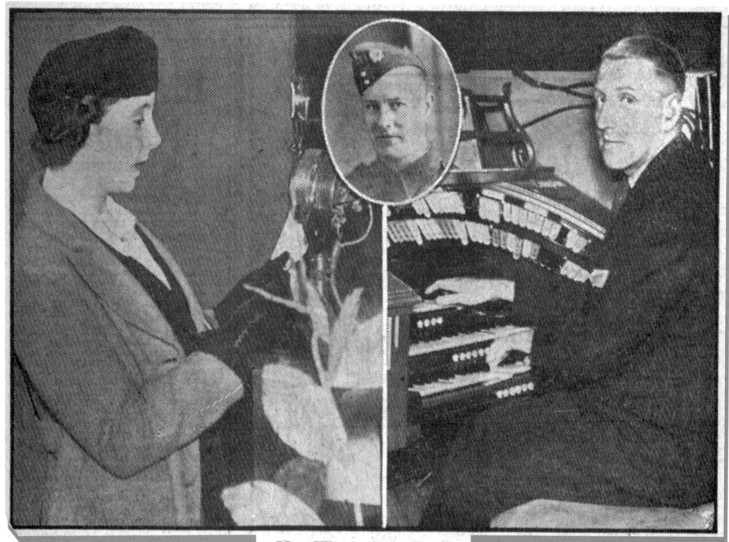

Mrs Winnie Dey, Huntly, broadcasting a birthday message to her husband, Driver George A. Dey (inset) in the Middle East. On the right is Sandy Macpherson, B.B.C. organist, in whose "request" programme a number of North-east people broadcast to relatives from the Capitol Cinema, Aberdeen. ("Press and Journal" copyright).

ENTERTAINMENT

WARTIME RADIO

Throughout the war the wireless was a lifeline for information as well as being great entertainment. For many people the war was an experience they totally lived through the wireless, snatching whatever information they could about the the victories and defeats in battle and also what was happening in Britain as the air raids reached Blitz proportions.

Nightly the radio was switched on a few minutes before it was needed so that the valves could warm up and give as good a sound as was possible in those days. Regular bulletins such as "War Report" and "Into Battle" were vital listening because most families in Britain knew someone who was at the sharp end of the conflict.

As a precaution against a possible German invasion, news readers were encouraged to become much more familiar to the public so that their voices were too well known for any German occupier to use the BBC for its own announcements. They even started to introduce themselves by name instead of remaining anonymous as before.

In October 1940 Broadcasting House was the victim of a direct hit from a bomb while Bruce Belfrage was reading a news bulletin. The explosion could be clearly heard by the millions of listeners but he just kept going and that in itself reflected the spirit of the nation at that time.

There were the famous broadcasts by Churchill. In recent years it has been revealed that Churchill did not always make the broadcasts himself, an actor, Norman Shelley who later was one of the regulars in *The Archers*, sometimes acting as stand-in because Churchill was so busy.

However, the messages of determination and encouragement such as "We'll fight 'em on the beaches" and "This was their finest hour" strengthened the hearts of British people both active and non-active and made the resolve to fight to the end even more determined.

While Churchill was encouraging everyone and boosting morale, William Joyce was trying to do the exact opposite. In his role as Lord Haw-Haw, he broadcast on German radio and could be heard by both British troops and those at home. His messages were always captivating by clever use of humour and familiarity before he embarked on a message that was intended to undermine the morale of the allies and cause public dissatisfaction with the way the war was being handled.

The sheer fascination of listening to him attracted many thousands of people and there is no doubt that for some it was a heart-sinking experience.

Radio was also used to broadcast coded messages as well as general information and was a lifeline for knowledge that not only played a vital part in the manoeuvres of war but also gave the general public a running commentary on how we were doing and what more could be done to help – encouragement that ranged from digging for victory to keeping quiet about anything which could be deemed a security risk.

There is no doubt that the radio played a major part in keeping people informed of events and in broadcasting public service messages but it also served to keep a smile on the faces of the British people and to distract their minds from the woes of war.

The highlight of each week was *ITMA – It's That Man Again –* which was broadcast at 8.30pm every Thursday. Tommy Handley was the man in question but he was aided and abetted by the likes of Maurice Denham, Jack Train, Deryck Guyler, Hattie Jacques, Molly Weir, Clarence Wright and Fred Yule.

Clarence Wright once recalled, "Tommy was a highly inventive performer, a humble man with his thoughts concentrated at that time on *ITMA*. He always felt that the next show had to be better than the last no matter how good it had been. When the *ITMA* door closed for the last time, Tommy left many happy and pleasant memories and, thankfully, a number of recordings."

Typical of the humour was Tommy Handley talking about a concert by his fictitious new orchestra.

"We played all the classics: 'The Charge of the Laundry' by Liszt; Beethoven's 'Too Ripe Tomato', Elgar's 'Circumpump and Stance', Offenbach's 'Horses' and 'Knees Up Mother Brahms.'

Mrs Mopp's catchphrase "Can I do you now sir?" is one of the legendary lines in radio history.

Hi Gang with Bebe Daniels, Ben Lyon and Vic Oliver was another of those comedy shows which meant so much to the listeners of the day as did *Bandwagon* with Arthur Askey and Richard Murdoch.

Ben Lyon and his wife, Bebe, were much-loved and respected by the British wireless listeners because they were American and could have left the country when the war hotted up. Instead they chose to remain in London and face the Blitz shoulder-to-shoulder with the Brits whom they had befriended. Britain never forgot their courageous stand against Hitler's attacks.

Arthur Askey once told me, "*Bandwagon* and other radio shows kept Britain laughing at a time when crying was much easier. I enjoyed doing the broadcasts and shows during those days and felt that I was adding something to the war effort. Let's face it, with me being about 5ft tall, I could hardly carry a pea–shooter, let alone a rifle on my back. I've seen bayonets taller than me.

Getting back to normal – Frank Dunlop (left) o, Aberdeen and "Tiger Shaw of Rangers lea their teams out a Hampden in the 1945-4 Scottish League Cup Fina

"So I kept myself busy – like the well-known bee – and tried to keep the nation laughing at Hitler. The wireless was great because you could picture all those families sitting round the fire, listening to the songs and the laughter and the news bulletins, not knowing what tomorrow was going to bring. For just a little while you could help them not to even care what tomorrow would bring."

It wasn't all news and laughs on the wireless. Serious programmes like *The Brains Trust* continued to discuss such grave topics as why you can't tickle yourself and other scientific mysteries. There were serious dramas too.

There was always room for a sing-song though and the music programmes pulled in huge listening figures whether they were the daytime *Music While You Work* programmes or evening shows featuring such familiar voices as Vera Lynn.

Just as listeners could not get too much information, they also could not get too much Vera Lynn and other singers.

Fighting back the tears many a family joined in with "We'll Meet Again" as they sat around the wireless during these difficult times.

VERA LYNN

Wars have scarred the history of mankind since his earliest beginnings and probably never so devastatingly as in the last hundred years. Amid the death and destruction though, heroes rise from the ashes. Some are noted for their acts of bravery, others for keeping a smile of hope on the faces of those who would otherwise be victims of despair. Such a person is a very special hero of World War Two, Dame Vera Lynn

They still call her The Forces' Sweetheart and Dame Vera Lynn not only lives up to that affectionate title but also, as she joins in remembering those fallen in conflict, shows the same fighting spirit which led Britain through the days of darkness back into the light of supposed peace.

One event Dame Vera Lynn has rarely missed is the annual Festival of Remembrance at the Royal Albert Hall in London.

"I don't like to miss that, it means a great deal to a lot of people, me included. It is not just about the World Wars of the 20th century but all the other wars including those still going on."

Dame Vera comes from a very British background, a family of people who liked to live life to the full.

"I was brought up in East London in a family of four including my brother Roger and my mum and dad of course. Although I was singing in local social clubs at the age of seven and enjoyed performing even for an audience of just one of my friends, I was always taught to keep my feet on the ground.

"My dad was an ordinary chap but spent a lot of his time at a nearby social club where he was involved in the entertainment and acted as MC for the dances. I was really proud when I first saw him performing that duty. My Uncle George, my dad's brother, also loved entertainment and sang in the clubs. He taught me a number of songs.

"Still, I was not pushed into entertaining but I was taught that there is more to life than performing and never to lose track of your roots and the everyday events of life. I don't think that was ever brought home to me any more than during the years of World War Two."

It was not only her superb voice and meaningful songs like "White Cliffs of Dover" and "We'll Meet Again" that made her such a popular star but it was also her down-to-earth personality, the girl-next-door character which meant so much to British people undergoing the pressure of war.

"When war broke out I heard about it on the radio like most people," she said. "It was expected but everyone hoped it could be avoided. It was quite chilling when the worst news was confirmed. My career was starting to go well and one of my first thoughts was that the war would end it.

"I went along to sign on for the army or whatever and I was told that I would be of much greater use if I carried on entertaining. I never thought that there was going to be much in the way of entertainment while there was a war on but I did as I was told and I am jolly glad I did."

The nation was pretty glad too because Vera Lynn became one of the icons of morale.

"It was a newspaper that ran a Forces' Sweetheart competition early in the war years," she recalled.

"I think the idea was to give the boys something else to think about as they started to go into France. I was really surprised when I was told that they had picked me. I had been getting good fan mail but to be voted above American singers who were so popular at the time was just amazing. I was really touched."

That image of the girl next door was a genuine one and has remained with Dame Vera throughout her life. Despite her years, she retains a youthful approach to life and has warmth and a ready smile for everyone she meets.

Vera Lynn,
The Forces'
Sweetheart

WARTIME FILMS

Neon signs were switched off as the nightly black out turned our cities into dwellings of darkness in an attempt to confuse the enemy bombers prowling through our skies. But while the names were no longer in bright lights, the celluloid stars still brought us romance, suspense and adventure at the local picture houses and the crowds flocked nightly to get away from the worries of war and escape to the fantasyland of the film world.

Cinemas ranged in standard from the comparatively plush Essoldo, Odeon, Gaumont and Colliseum to the local 'flea-pit'. The films themselves also were wide-ranging in quality. At the very start of the war in 1939, *Gone With The Wind* stole the show. It was much awaited and Clarke Gable and Vivien Leigh did not disappoint.

Many a female heart fluttered as Gable gave that special smouldering look and uttered those immortal words, "Frankly, my dear, I don't give a damn." That was stern stuff in 1939 though tame today. It was not so much the words but the delivery of them.

Gone With The Wind remains a firm favourite today, a film legend that did much to capture the hearts and minds of the public who had their hearts in their mouths as the early fires of war consumed fresh kindling on its way to becoming a world-wide blaze.

With eight Academy Awards, box office records and an amazing 220 minutes of non-stop drama, *Gone With the Wind* is one of the greatest films of all time.

1939 was quite a year because another legend of film history also came to life on the big screen. It started in black and white and blossomed into full colour, it included a lion, a scarecrow, a tin man and a little girl and her dog. Yes, 1939 was also the year of the *Wizard of Oz* with Judy Garland and the gang singing and dancing their way along the yellow brick road to the delight of tens of millions of cinema-goers then and the rest of us today.

The Great Dictator was one of the first and most enduring of the propaganda films. Charlie Chaplin excelled in some very funny scenes which seriously poked fun at the Hitler–Mussolini relationship and gave everyone a chance to laugh their fears away. That was in 1940 and in that same year there was another ground-breaking release by Disney as the brilliant *Fantasia* reached the screen. It was breathtakingly clever with humour and beauty along with some of the world's finest music. Who could ever forget the "Sorcerer's Apprentice" with Mickey Mouse starring?

The wartime films we remember and sometimes see on television include classics like *Citizen Kane* with Orson Welles who both directed and starred in it. That was a 1941 film and one we have all heard of yet there was another which was more of a morale booster. It was called *Forty-Ninth Parallel* although sometimes titled *The Invaders*. It told the tale of survivors from a sunk German U-boat on the run in Canada. Laurence Olivier, Leslie Howard, Raymond Massey, Eric Portman and Glynis Johns starred and it proved to be quite a thriller. With such names on the cast list it proved to be big box office too.

The morale machine moved into overdrive as favourites of the day combined forces to put a smile on the faces of those under pressure and to drive home the message that the allies would prevail. Basil Rathbone moved his Sherlock Holmes character well out of his normal Victorian environment to cross swords with the Nazis and the Crazy Gang did their bit for the war effort in *Gas Bags* which saw them steal a German secret weapon. Who could forget Will Hay starring in *The Goose Steps Out* when he taught German students how to make a two-fingers rampant salute to Der Führer?

The classics continued to roll out. Disney gave us *Bambi* in 1942. while Humphrey Bogart and Ingrid Bergman sizzled in the heat of *Casablanca*, one film which we have played again and again with or without Sam. As if that was not enough, there was the classic *Mrs Minever* which won seven Academy Awards and told the everyday tale of London folk during the difficulties of war. Greer Garson, Walter Pidgeon and Richard Ney starred and at the same time cinema-goers were treated to *In Which we Serve*, a naval story of wartime courage at sea. It starred the unique Mr Noel Coward. Errol Flynn starred as an escaping POW in *Desperate Journey*, cheered on by packed cinema audiences all over the allied world.

For Whom the Bell Tolls was the classic of 1943 and once again Ingrid Bergman proved to be big box office as she starred with Gary Cooper. It was the biggest movie of the year but a close second was *Jane Eyre* with Orson Welles and Joan Fontaine, possibly the best film version ever made.

Double Indemnity came the following year and provided a hugely popular vehicle for Fred MacMurray, Barbara Stanwyck and Edward G. Robinson. Perhaps the biggest film of that year though was one of those which lifted the spirits with its all-singing approach to life. Judy Garland starred in *Meet Me in St. Louis* and dealt a dose of optimism to everyone that went to see it.

The propaganda films continued to flow throughout the war and of course, the Allies were always the heroes and the Germans and their friends were always the villains or objects of ridicule. There would not be much point to propaganda if that was not the case.

At last the war was over in 1945 and if anything the cinemas were even busier. The war films continued but so did all the other classics including Alfred Hitchcock's thriller *Spellbound* with Gregory Peck and Ingrid Bergman who became quite the star of the war-time classics.

Yes, the neon lights were blacked out but the stars shone as brightly as ever to keep the spirits high during World War Two.

ENTERTAINERS AT WAR

When war broke out many men and women enlisted into the armed forces but many more were turned away because the jobs they already did contributed to the war effort. Some of those were our entertainers who could offer more in boosting morale by doing what they did best than in picking up a rifle.

Max Miller was almost resident at the Holborn Empire in London until it was bombed in 1940. When not there he spent much of his time at the London Palladium, topping the bill week after week and playing to audiences of people carrying gas masks, many of them in the uniforms of the various services. He offered light relief from the dismal demolition that went on around the country as Hitler's bombs crashed to the ground most nights.

"Max was a bill topper well before the war started and what he offered was total escape," said Roy Hudd. "He was well known for laughing in the face of the censors and the more risqué he went, the more the audiences loved him. He was never blue in today's sense but said more by what he didn't actually say than what he did say. He was a genius in the real sense and during the war he often gave up his time to entertain the troops and his audiences

Noel Coward, the famous actor, playwright and producer, is welcomed by Mr T. Loudon, stationmaster, on his arrival at Aberdeen in December 1942

were always full of soldiers, sailors and airmen and their girlfriends and wives. He made them feel good."

If Max Miller was at home in London, George Formby was certainly at home in Blackpool and during the 1930s and 1940s he packed audiences into theatres there with his own special brand of song and humour. But he took the war effort very seriously and made a number of trips to the front line to entertain the troops. On one occasion he heard that there were British troops entrenched just a few yards from enemy lines. He urged officers to let him go and say hello and did so without once thinking of the risk he was taking. He was told to leave his ukulele behind though just in case he was tempted to give a quick rendition of "We're going to hang out our washing on the Siegfried Line".

Gracie Fields came in for some criticism during the war when she left with her husband to live in America. Previously she had been a national heroine but when the news broke of her taking off to the States, public opinion moved against her for a while. However, she did return to France and to North Africa and later to the Pacific to entertain the troops so she did play her part in keeping the spirits up during the conflict.

Flanagan and Allen possibly enjoyed their finest hour during the war. They were popular for years before and after the conflict but during those dark days their songs and fun kept Britain laughing and humming along, especially when the rest of the Crazy Gang were involved. Bud and Ches were also used quite a lot for public service films during the war, the government seeing them as ideal entertainers to deliver important messages. They were quite right, whenever Bud Flanagan and Chesney Allen spoke or sang, millions listened.

Sir Harry Lauder topped the bill at many fund-raising events and on more than one occasion he was joined by a young lad who went on to much greater things. Jimmy Logan never forgot his shows with Harry Lauder, his hero. Meanwhile, Glasgow's Theatre Royal was home to comedy star Dave Willis who kept up the wartime spirits in pantomime and summer variety shows. During World War Two another great Scots comedy star Lex McLean was in charge of the first ENSA company and he visited army units all over Scotland. Most entertainers did their bit during the war in one way or another. Tommy Trinder, Sandy Powell, Jimmy Wheeler, Norman Evans, Robb Wilton, Arthur Askey and of course Vera Lynn were among those who found themselves constantly in demand at theatres and by the military chiefs who were keen to take advantage of their appeal to send them off to entertain the troops.

"You never knew where you were going," said Vera Lynn. You just found yourself in the back of a truck and going somewhere. Even when you got there you often didn't know where you were. But you just got on with it and did your best to entertain and cheer everyone up. You always felt appreciated though and that made it all worth while."

BRITAIN AT WAR
DID YOU KNOW?

NORMAN WISDOM was assigned to the Royal Corps of Signals during the war and spent some of his time seconded to a top–secret wartime communications post.

"I saw quite a bit of Churchill," he said. "He even knew me by name and would often enquire if everything was all right. You had to reply in a direct style and could never try to engage him in unnecessary conversation."

JON PERTWEE really was in the navy and had an amazing number of life-threatening escapes including being aboard HMS *Hood* just before it was to sail to find and destroy the *Bismarck*. Jon was summoned for a special assignment and left the ship only hours before it sailed into a disaster that claimed the lives of all but three of the more than 1,400 crew in board.

KENNETH MOORE might have been acclaimed for his portrayal of Sir Douglas Bader in *Reach For The Sky* but during the war he actually served in the Royal Navy.

THE BEVERLEY SISTERS were asked by the BBC to audition at a secret underground studio in Bedford.

"It was very exciting," said Teddie. "It became even more exciting when a man walked in to listen to us. We couldn't believe it because he was none other than Glenn Miller. He was unbelievably kind to us even though we were just three scruffy little evacuees from London.

"He really changed our lives and set us on the road to fame. He told us we had passed our audition and offered to help in any way he could. Since we had no accompaniment of our own, he made his rhythm section available to us and they actually backed us on our early broadcasts. He was so nice that we were all heartbroken when he went missing. We have never forgotten him though and always try to include one of his numbers in our programme."

THE LONDON PALLADIUM did not emerge unscathed as a parachute bomb smashed through the roof and suspend itself over the wings, still live. A naval office defused it and the show went on as planned. The officer was given two tickets for the Palladium for life.

Mr Harry Gordon,
the well known
Aberdeen comedian

His Majesty's Theatre, Aberdeen
PROPRIETORS—
JAMES F. DONALD (Aberdeen Cinemas) LTD.
Manager - - - - J. R. DONALD.

PROGRAMME

WEEK COMMENCING MONDAY, 4th MAY, 1942
Twice Nightly at 6.30 and 8.30.

Aberdeen's Very Own Star Comedian and Radio Favourite:
HARRY GORDON
In **SECOND EDITION** of
"LAFFTIME"
WITH FULL VARIETY COMPANY
. . including . .
JACK HOLDEN   HILDA MEACHAM
Arthur Clarke   Gwyneth Lascelles   Alex. Lennox
THE FOUR GORDON TILLER GIRLS
MADAME TRUZZI
LAURIE MELLIN
THE TEN VICTORIA GIRLS
"MELODY FOR YOU" with JEANNE GAYE, MOYA & ROY

O.S., 3/-; D.C., 2/6; P.S., 2/-; C., 1/6; B.S., 1/-; Bal., 7d.

Box Office—9.30 a.m. to 9.30 p.m.   Telephone 493.
The Management reserve the right to make any alterations in the cast owing to illness or other unavoidable circumstances.
The Management reserve the right to refuse admission.
N.B.—Seats reserved by Telephone are not guaranteed until paid for, and will not be kept after all other seats for that part of the Theatre have been sold.

The Press and Journal

Sold Everywhere 1/1 and 1/10½d.

No. 28,289. 198th Year. 1½d.

SATURDAY, SEPTEMBER 1, 1945

A KEMSLEY NEWSPAPER.

ROYAL SCOTS FREED FROM JAP PRISON CAMPS

Grim Tales of Ordeal: Pilfered Food To Eke Out Meagre Diet

JOY AT SURRENDER NEWS

From DAVID DIVINE, "The Press and Journal" War Correspondent,
On board U.S. Hospital Ship Benevolence

OFF TOKIO, Thursday.

WITHIN sight of the dome of the Japanese Parliament buildings we have been watching all afternoon boatloads of cheering prisoners of war coming out from the hell of Japanese prison camps.

The first and most-lasting impression is one of gaiety—gaiety that brings a lump to the throat—as men, wet to the skin from the choppy sea, haggard, clothed often enough in rags, emaciated and ill, cheer, shout and wave to their luckier comrades already on the decks of the hospital ship.

Many of them are wearing gaudy scarves, arm-bands and head decorations of the scarlet and orange material of parachutes used in dropping food containers to the camps.

On board the U.S.S. Benevolence the greater proportion of the men were British—men of the Royal Scots and Middlesex Regiment, Midlanders, Welshmen, and Australians.

The Merchant Navy had representatives of half the ports of the United Kingdom.

There were men from Hong-Kong and Shanghai, men captured by German raiders before Japan came into the war, and men shot down from British carrier planes in the last weeks of Admiral Halsey's last and greatest stroke against the Japanese Empire.

CAPTURED AT HONG-KONG

The grim honour of seniority among the prisoners interviewed belong to men of the Royal Scots and Middlesex Regiment captured in Hong-Kong in the harsh December, 1941.

THE WAR IN THE EAST

NOT FORGETTING JAPAN

While conflict raged in Europe, on another stage there was another phase of World War Two and Gordon Highlander Jimmy Scott knew the horrors of both scenarios.

As north-east soldier Jimmy Scott buried the burned corpses of his comrades, he knew he too was facing a similar terrifying end. Many had been mercilessly tortured by their Japanese captors. Others died from starvation, botched amputations and terrible illnesses suffered while working on the notorious Burma death railway and its Bridge over the River Kwai.

In his most desperate hour, Jimmy never dreamed that 60 years later, he would be safe in Turriff, a survivor standing before a monument and remembering those who had fallen.

Born in Cuminestown, Jimmy was in the Territorial Army when World War Two broke out and he was immediately called up to join the 6th Battalion Gordon Highlanders.

They were shipped to France to reinforce the 1st Battalion Gordon Highlanders but the German onslaught was too great and the British forces retreated to Dunkirk.

Jimmy managed to clamber on board one of the rescue ships but, about a mile out, it was attacked by German warplanes. Sheltering under some pipes on the deck, Jimmy was hit by a piece of shrapnel and he spent seven weeks in hospital. However, after a fortnight's leave at Bridge of Don Barracks, Jimmy was declared fit for active duty.

His next posting was with the 2nd Battalion Gordon Highlanders in Singapore. He had not been there very long though when the Japanese invaded and allied forces surrendered on February 15, 1942.

That was when the true horror began.

Jimmy remembered, "They raided the Alexandra Hospital, shooting, stabbing or bayoneting all the patients, military and civilians and any medical staff who protested.

"Then they got a mechanical digger, dug a hole, threw the bodies in – some not even dead – and filled the hole up.

"All girls aged six to 18 were sheltered in a big mosque to try to save them but very few escaped those animals."

As a POW he was put to work building the notorious Railway of Death.

"We started clearing a strip through the jungle, cutting down trees and levelling out a track back towards the River Kwai," said Jimmy.

"There were no barrows to move the earth, we had to use a carrier, like a stretcher."

The men using the carriers were called runners. Jimmy explained, "You had to move at a sort of a trot. If you didn't trot they belted you with stones or their rifles.

"When we reached the River Kwai there had to be a bridge built over it. Of course it became a famous film and while some of it depicts the reality quite well I don't think it really captures the horrible feeling of actually being there.

"Hundreds of lives were lost either by falling into the river and being swept away or through weakness or tropical diseases like cholera, beri beri, dysentery or malaria."

He told how men were forced to drill through hard rock by hand and, starving, how they ate dogs and snails and bred rats to eat.

"We were getting weaker all the time and it became too time consuming burying the dead.

"They made us build huge fires and the bodies were thrown on to these fires and cremated, after they had removed any rings or false teeth."

Medical treatment was basic – or non existent.

"If your skin got cut by bamboo or a chip from the rock, the sore usually turned into a tropical ulcer. These ulcers grew bigger and bigger sometimes with a whole hip or calf of a leg eaten away," said Jimmy.

"Limbs had to be amputated and this was done by a joiner's saw."

Several prisoners tried to escape – but the punishment was severe.

"One form was to put them up against a tree, tie wire round their fingers and wrists on one arm, hold them up clear of the ground, wind the wire round the tree twice, then round the fingers and wrist of the other arm and leave them hanging there for the night.

"We could hear them screaming but couldn't do anything to help," he said.

Ironically his own life was probably saved by a Japanese medical officer.

When Jimmy fell ill with diphtheria the officer sent him back to hospital in the Changi camp in Singapore.

"I was down to six-and-a-half stone and had to lie on my right side to be able to swallow because of a hole that had developed on the left side of my throat."

Jimmy's torment lasted for a total of three-and-a-half years until liberation finally came while he was at Changi.

When he returned to the north-east he worked at Turriff's Crichton and Sons, manufacturing threshing mills, then was a BT engineer for 29 years until he retired.

He is a stalwart of the Royal British Legion and in 1998 was rewarded for his services with an MBE. But it is a rare day that his memories do not come flooding back, recalling his fallen comrades.

FACING A KAMIKAZE PILOT

The Japanese kamikaze plane came out of nowhere and screamed towards the HMS *Formidable* before slamming into its armoured flight deck. A young Aberdeen gunner watched helplessly as his friend was blown in two.

For 84-year-old George Hulse, of Seaton, Aberdeen, the hellish experience of 60 years ago lived vividly in his memory for ever.

George was an acting Leading Seaman at the time of the attack on May 4, 1945.

The aircraft carrier HMS *Formidable* was part of the British Pacific Fleet launching air strikes against Sakishima Gunto, a group of Japanese islands.

Though in its death throes, the Japanese Empire was still fighting hard – including swarms of the dreaded kamikaze suicide planes.

George, who was manning one of *Formidable's* Mark 14 anti-aircraft guns on the day said, "They were coming at us from all different angles.

"Some of them were just crashing into the sea without even being hit.

"They targeted the bridge because that was where they could cause most damage."

Most of the time the gunners picked off the planes before they struck, but there were too many.

George said, "The one that got through came out of nowhere. It couldn't be stopped."

The impact shook the aircraft carrier and a friend, who was two yards away, was torn in two by the blast.

"You can't dream of such a thing. Part of him was in one place and the rest in another," said the former building site warden.

The navy's official record says eight men died that day. George remembers it differently.

He said, "I heard that there were about 90 dead and from what I saw with my own eyes I have never had any reason to doubt it.

"It was like a little bit of hell."

A piece of metal plate was welded over the dent in the flight deck where the kamikaze's 500lb bomb had left a two-foot hole in the thick armour.

HMS *Formidable* was ready for action again in just five hours.

George was physically unmarked by the experience but he was left shaking for hours, despite a nerve-steadying tot of rum prescribed by the ship's doctor.

George had witnessed his share of death and injury since joining the Royal Navy in 1937.

He saw service during the Norwegian campaign and on minesweepers protecting the Atlantic convoys.

Picking up survivors from sunken ships provided more harrowing memories.

He recalls a survivor who was plucked from the water who had more 50 per cent burns after swimming through flaming oil.

Press and Journal

No. 27,127, 194th Year   ABERDEEN, TUESDAY, DECEMBER 9, 1941   THREE HALFPENCE

Price 1/6

BRITAIN AND U.S. DECLARE WAR ON JAPAN

British Forces in Action in Malaya

BOMBING OF MANILA RESUMED

BRITAIN and America have formally declared war on Japan.

Britain's declaration was made at 1 p.m. yesterday, and was announced by the Premier in the House of Commons.

The formal United States declaration was made at 8.28 p.m. (B.S.T.).

The resolution was passed by the Senate by 82 votes to none. The House passed it by 388 votes to 1. Sole dissenter was the Republican pacifist, Miss Jeannette Rankin. Fifty voted against war with Germany in 1917.

While Japanese aircraft have resumed the bombing of American bases in the Pacific, the most serious enemy drive is believed to be against Thailand. Reports from there are unfortunately meagre.

British reconnaissance has disclosed that the Japanese made two landings in the Kra Isthmus, just north of the Malay border—at Patani and Singora.

From these points they presumably hope swiftly to occupy the whole narrow isthmus, thus cutting direct communications between Malaya and Thailand, so as to reduce the possibility of support for Thailand from Malaya.

An official announcement quoted by Bangkok radio last night confirmed that, following the Japanese invasion, the "Cease Fire" has been ordered in Thailand, and the Thai Cabinet has decided to accept the Japanese terms the passage of Japanese troops through the country while Japan has to respect Thai

George said, "His skin was just coming off and with that amount of burns he wasn't going to live."

George added, "I saw some terrible things. The ship being hit by a kamikaze was the worst.

"But I wouldn't want anybody to think it was all like that.

"There were good times, too, particularly the comradeship," he said.

"In fact, the good times back then were probably the best of my life."

THE REMARKABLE WILLIE CHISHOLM

For many years the remarkable story of Willie Chisholm had never been told. Yet the life of the quiet country boy from Aberdeenshire could be the stuff of films.

Captured with his wife and two little daughters, he spent nearly three years in a brutal Japanese prisoner-of-war camp.

Then, soon after arriving back in Aberdeen when peace was declared, Willie was asked by the Foreign Office to take on a special mission in defeated and battle-scarred Berlin.

Thanks to his fluent German, he was appointed deputy governor of the now legendary Spandau jail.

There he was charged with guarding Adolf Hitler's most notorious generals, including Rudolf Hess.

The men became chess-mates and companions.

And when Willie died, the former Deputy Führer of the Nazi Party – who was by then the only prisoner left in Spandau – was grief-stricken.

Yet Willie's life was never been recorded, even when he was made a MBE for his work in Spandau.

He was born in Lumphanan in 1901, went to the local school and then to work in a sawmill.

Always passionate about seeing the world, Willie joined the Shanghai Police in China when he was just 18.

Later he became one of the top officers at the nearby prison.

Willie regularly kept in touch with his friends back home in Aberdeenshire, including David MacRae, a young prison officer in Peterhead.

However, David died tragically from pneumonia when he was just 25, leaving his young wife, Ina, with a three-month-old daughter, Moira.

On a visit home, Willie and Ina fell in love and in 1935 the newlyweds and the baby set off again for Shanghai.

The next year Ina gave birth to a second daughter, Rona. However, the days of their idyllic life were numbered.

The storm clouds were gathering. Europe was plunged into World War Two.

After Pearl Harbour was bombed in 1941, the Chisholms' life dramatically changed.

They were all issued with identity cards and curfews were imposed on when they could leave their houses.

Willie's daughter Moira, who was nine at the time, said, "I knew something bad was going on because I would hear my parents talking to others and then stop when I came into the room.

"Then one day in February, 1943, that I'll never forget, the Japanese knocked at the door.

"We were allowed a case each and a bed between us, then we were loaded on to a truck and driven to a prison camp.

"I wasn't scared. I was all right as long as Mum, Dad and my sister Rona were with me.

"We were lucky we were kept together the whole time. I think that's how we managed to survive."

At their first camp, the Chisholms slept with other families in an old school, with proper toilets.

But after a year they were moved to a rat-infested compound of huts – 24 people in each – with nothing but trenches in the earth for lavatories.

Their daily ration of food was a handful of rice or fish.

Moira said, "Sometimes the guards would try to play games with the children. But I wasn't scared of them so I'd just scream at them to stay away from us.

"When I had to get a tooth pulled, my mother was begging the dentist to give me an injection.

"Then the guard started hitting her, so I jumped up and started hitting him as well.

"One of the guards was really kind to me. I think his daughter had died.

"He used to say he wanted to take me home to be with his wife and son.

"I said my mum would never let me go. But she said she would – if it meant saving my life."

With Willie's care and protection, and their individual bravery and stoicism, the family survived their long ordeal.

One memorable day in August 1945, Moira – then aged 12 – heard shouting and cheering from outside the compound fence.

She said, "I ran out and heard the huge crowd of Chinese chanting something.

"I could speak some of the language and realised they were saying the war was over, so I ran in and told my mum and dad.

"It was a wonderful feeling to be free again and by the next month we were back in Aberdeen.

"But I still get flashbacks to that camp nearly 60 years later."

VJ night and there are bonfires in the streets

D-DAY AND BEYOND

D-DAY AT LAST

Scotland's own were among the thick of the fighting on that historic and dangerous day on June 6, 1944.

As reported in the *Press & Journal* shortly after the event, a German officer said, "We had gone to ground and had emerged only to find ourselves surrounded by tanks and furious Scotsmen throwing grenades."

There were numerous Scottish units and formations involved in the action from June 6 to 12, as well as individual Scots who were in other regiments and those with Scottish roots, such as the Canadian units.

The 1st Battalion King's Own Scottish Borderers landed on June 6 on beach area Sword as part of the 9th Brigade of the 3rd Infantry Division.

The beach area Juno saw landings by the 153rd Brigade of the 51st Highland Division comprising the 1st Battalion Gordon Highlanders, 5/7th Battalion Gordon Highlanders and 5th Battalion Black Watch.

The Royal Scots Greys landed on June 7 and 8 as part of the Armoured Brigade.

Between June 7 and 9 the 152nd Brigade of the 51st Highland Division comprising 5th Battalion Cameron Highlanders and 2/5 Battalion Seaforth Highlanders landed on the beaches.

There were many Scottish individuals who were in action while serving with the RAF, the Royal Navy, the Merchant Navy and the nursing sections.

The Royal Navy and the RAF were not organised on a regional basis with the exception of 602 (City of Glasgow) Squadron, RAF, one of several pre-war Scottish squadrons of the Royal Auxiliary Air Force which had been mobilised. As part of the 25th Wing of the 2nd Tactical Air Force, 602 provided low-level fighter cover over beach area Utah.

In addition to the legendary commando leader Lord Lovat, who famously ordered his piper Bill Millin to play on the beach, various other Scottish military heroes led the way to freedom on D-Day.

Admiral Sir Bertram Home Ramsay was Naval Commander Allied Expeditionary Force for the invasion of Europe. He was responsible for planning and carrying out Operation Neptune, the naval element of the landings. Admiral Ramsay was killed in a plane crash in January 1945.

Major General T. G. Rennie commanded the 3rd Infantry Division, one of the two

Crowds in Castle Street, Aberdeen, August 19, 1945. The Lord Provost surveys the scene

Celebrations in the streets,
August 15, 1945

British assault divisions on D-Day. He later took command of the 51st Highland Division and was killed in action in March 1945.

Major General D. Graham commanded the 50th Infantry Division, the other British assault division while Brigadier A. S. Pearson commanded the 8th Battalion the Parachute Regiment as part of the 6th Airborne Division. Brigadier Pearson was remarkable in having been awarded three bars to his DSO, making him one of the most decorated soldiers of the war.

Group Captain J.M. Stagg also merits a mention since he was General Eisenhower's chief meteorological adviser.

Pre-invasion training in Scotland took place at Kirkcudbright, Inverary, Easter Ross, the Moray Firth, Loch Striven and Port Bannatyne Bay, the Isle of Arran, Loch Fyne and Scapa Flow, Roseneath and Gareloch, Achnacarry and Rigg Bay, Isle of Whithorn.

At the end of June 1944 the 15th Scottish Division under Maj.-Gen. G. H. A. MacMillan drove towards the bridges of the River Odon and had what was reported to be a "devastating effect". Their route became known as the Scottish Corridor, a tribute indeed to the contribution of the "furious Scotsmen".

Jimmy Clark was 19 when he went into battle on D-Day along with his comrades in Lord Lovat's band of heroes. The Glaswegian who now lives on Skye remembers well that day in 1944 when lives were lost but victory was gained.

"I was an apprentice draughtsman before I volunteered for the army and went through the same vigorous training as everyone else in that elite band of commandos.

"We crossed the channel on what seemed a very rough sea. We knew it was going to be make or break although we had every confidence it was going to be successful.

"There were few of us who were not seasick so our relief at getting under way was nothing as compared with our relief at seeing land. We could not get off that boat fast enough even though we had to wade some distance while we were under fire. Our vessel took a direct hit just after most of us had disembarked.

"Jerry gave us a pelting and many fell even before they could fight back. Despite that we met our objective which was to meet up with 6th Airborne.

"I can remember running across Pegasus Bridge with Lord Lovat having already gone ahead with his piper, Bill Millin, playing 'Blue Bonnets over the Border'. It made a big difference to us to hear the pipes. I am sure it steeled our determination.

"On the other side of the bridge Lord Lovat spoke to each one of us, looked at the number on our shoulder and directed us. I can see him now with his rifle slung over his shoulder and his stick in his hand.

"We dug in at one end of a large apple orchard. The Germans were at the other end. Even in a situation like that there was something to bring a smile. A really large pig ran out

Celebrating peace was worth a few risks

Wings for Victory Week parade, Union Street, Aberdeen, June 19, 1943

in front of us. It was about halfway between the two lines and one of our men shot it.

"To our surprise two Germans wearing Red Cross armbands ran out from their ranks, put the pig on a stretcher and made off with it! We did not know whether to laugh or feel cheated."

Jimmy was wounded in the chest a few days later and sent back to England for treatment. He later rejoined Lord Lovat for the remainder of the war.

After the war Jimmy could not settle in civilian life and joined the Queen's Own Cameron Highlanders serving in the Middle East. Later he joined the Argyll and Sutherland Highlanders before going back to the Camerons.

"I had 16 years in all and saw plenty of action but there was nothing quite like D-Day," said Jimmy. "I take out my medals every year and think of those who deserved them but were never able to wear them."

Amid the noise of battle there was one unmistakable sound like no other and Tom Duncan of Cruden Bay remembers well the skirl of the bagpipes as Lord Lovat's piper, Bill Millin, inspired the charge to deliver France on D-Day.

Tom was in an elite troop of commandos, a part of the legendary Lord Lovat's 1st Special Services Brigade which had gained celebrity status in the forces after successes in action throughout Europe and the Middle East.

The Aberdeen Journals office join in the victory celebrations

"To earn the coveted commando green beret, every selected volunteer had to pass a three-month training course at Achnacarry," he recalled. "This was no ordinary course. Anyone of rank was stripped of their stripes at the start to give everyone a level base. I was on attachment from the Gordon Highlanders.

"Lord Lovat was a charismatic leader and most men would have followed him wherever he led. He knew about battle and he knew about men and how to get the best out of them. We had specialist instructors, live ammunition and were confined to barracks. Everything was designed to make it as tough as possible.

"Later we were moved to the south coast for more training which included street fighting in London. We had already learned a lot from stalking deer in Scotland, but now we were getting down to the face to face stuff. We also had intensive training in landing craft.

The VJ Sunday parade at the junction of Back Wynd and Union Street in Aberdeen city centre

"Everyone knew the invasion was near but nobody knew when it would be and we had to concentrate on keeping 100% fit. We had a visit from Field Marshall Montgomery who stood on his jeep to address us so we knew that the day was very close indeed."

Then D-day finally dawned.

"We had been allocated two landing craft and crossed the channel in them with our faces blackened in preparation for a dawn landing," he recalled. "We were well armed and keyed up for the battle ahead. Some joker then washed himself and started to have a shave so we all joined in the joke and did the same. We must have been the cleanest troops on the beach that day.

"We were among the first to land but there had already been a previous wave of troops and as we landed the beach was under small arms fire and continuous shell fire," he recalled. "There were some of our early troops on the beach with shocking injuries, most of the casualties resulting from mortar bombs which were screaming down like flocks of partridges.

"Our mortar troop on the right were blown sky high by a direct hit from a shell as they were coming in to land. Our sergeant major was hit and fell back into the boat wounded. He was returned safely to England without ever disembarking."

Although the fighting was fierce, the Allies gradually began to gain ground.

"Those of us who got off the beach met up in a swamp beyond the beach head. I remember our Colonel, Peter Young, DSO and MC, flashing a smile and saying, 'Glad you came along Duncan'. It was a memorable moment, a typical British understatement.

"We also met up with a member of the French Resistance who brought us a bottle of wine and it was just too tempting for us not to have a swig each."

Amid the fierce fighting there was still communication between divisions.

"Word had been flashed to us that the 6th Airborne had captured the bridges over the River Orme on the extreme left flank of the 2nd Army. Our task was to fight our way through the enemy territory in between and reinforce the Airborne.

"We achieved that in three and a half hours but we were two and a half minutes late. Sometimes the fighting was savage and there were rarely any lulls. Cries of the wounded had to go unheeded. Fighting men were forbidden from stopping to give aid. Help would come later although for some it arrived too late.

"When we joined the 6th Airborne it was good to see the green berets of the commandos mingling with the red berets but there was another, more poignant sight during that first day. It was the scene in which British medical orderlies and those from Germany were working side by side to tend their fallen. They were almost shoulder to shoulder with only the saving of lives on their minds.

"We had seen some fearsome sights that day with horrendously wounded and dead scattered around us, men who had been talking to us and were now blown to bits.

"As I thought about those moments of the day that was now passing, a German grenade landed nearby and I was wounded and returned to England. I did go back though two months later taking the same route across the Normandy beaches and I am sure that I found the same hole in which I had dug in that night.

"I don't think you ever forget something like that," he said. "I think when you look back you realise other points which you probably did not fully appreciate at the time.

"I lost many good mates. One of my pals had a premonition he was going to cop it and told me we should never have landed in Normandy. He was dead within half an hour.

"Above all that, I shall never forget hearing the skirl of Bill Millin's pipes. It is hard to describe the impact it had. It gave us a great lift and increased our determination.

"As well as the pride we felt, it reminded us of home and why we were there fighting for our lives and those of our loved ones."

VE Day celebrations in Union Street, Aberdeen

FIRST INTO BELSEN

Anyone who denies the existence of the Holocaust needs their head examined, according to former Royal Engineer Fred Stevens of Aboyne. Fred should know – in 1945, he managed to unbolt the gate into Belsen, the notorious concentration camp, to be greeted by the sight of people dead and dying and a stench he will never forget.

Fred said, "When I went into the camp at Belsen, I saw people – if you can call walking skeletons people – I will see in my mind's eye forever. They had sticks for arms and legs. They tried to run towards me; they put those sticks around my neck and mumbled in Polish, I think it was.

"They had no stomachs and their eyes were sunken back into their heads.

"You couldn't tell if those skeletons were men or women. Put it this way – they didn't need X-rays to show me that their ribs had been broken.

"I remember the tall gates to the camp, covered in barbed wire. I remember the sergeant saying, 'Get that bloody gate open!' which we did with bolt-croppers.

"Belsen." He screws up his face at the pain of his memories.

"It was absolutely repulsive. I was 24 at the time and it was the worst thing I have ever seen in my life.

"Those people coming towards me, those emaciated skeletons. The smell was appalling. There were dead bodies everywhere. One minute you'd be talking to somebody and the next they would fall down and die. It was unbelievable that people could treat human beings in such a way."

Fred remembers being ordered to arrest a German woman called Irma, who was in charge of the women's camp.

"She was a cold, hard woman," he said. "We took her to the military police and I remember her spitting at one of the policemen."

Fred remembers the Sunday he was called up back in 1939.

"It was exciting, at the age of 17," he recalled. "We had to go to Brighton for training. Every morning, we'd don our rifles and kitbags and get on the bus to Brighton, saying, 'Right, we're off to fight the war.' Then we'd go back home at night and return the next day. We trained for about a month."

Reality hit only when Fred and his fellow conscripts were taken to Dover.

"I remember thinking, 'I wonder if I'll ever be back in Portslade again?'" he said.

Fred is a character. An adopted Scot, he still has a broad Sussex accent and punctuates his sentences with old-fashioned epithets such as "luvaduck" and "oh my Gawd".

With the Royal Engineers – the Ginger Beers he calls them – Fred spent most of his time mine-detecting. "I was the one in the headphones, waving a stick around," he said.

"As everybody knows, we were driven back by the Germans and returned to Dunkirk.

"We got on to a fishing boat and started making our way back to Dover, but the Germans bombed us and the boat sank.

"I do remember that. I remember my friend who was standing beside me suggesting we went and sat by the funnel at the front of the boat because it would be warmer there. They bombed the back of the boat and a lot of men were killed.

"I spent an hour in the water and was picked up eventually by HMS *Worcester*.

"We landed at Dover, went to Redhill then out to Africa to finish off the Germans," Fred said. "Then to Sicily and back to England."

At that point in his service, Fred was transferred to the 51st Highland Division.

"Marvellous blokes," he said.

He returned to France, "Luvaduck, I can't remember how long for."

It was then he was sent on his memorable mission, to Northern Germany, to a small village called Belsen.

A few years ago, Fred saw a letter in the *Press & Journal* signed by the commander of HMS *Worcester*. Fred wrote to him to thank him for having saved his life. The commander responded warmly, saying he remembered the bombing but could not remember individuals as there had been too many drowning men to rescue.

After a veritable torrent of "Lord, luvaducks", Fred managed to tell me that the boat-hook used in the rescue operation, which had been intended for his trousers, had accidentally pierced his backside.

"Gawd, that was painful," he exclaimed, adding, "I'll show you the scar, if you like."

But the never-ending nightmare the former engineer endures is the memory of being the first into Belsen.

THE LONE PIPER

Perhaps the true spirit of Scotland at war is summed up by one man, Bill Millin whose courage on D-Day has made him a legend.

As he played his bagpipes to inspire fellow commandos amid the slaughter of the Sword D-Day invasion beach, Bill Millin felt not a flicker of fear.

"I did not feel fear because I was occupied. I was lucky," recalled the modest 81-year-old as he relived the extraordinary musical episode that has become part of D-Day folklore over the decades.

The then 21-year-old piper could not have been more conspicuous in his kilt – unarmed apart from the dirk in his sock as he marched up and down the bullet torn beach playing, amongst others, the Scottish marching tune "Highland Laddie".

Around half the 1,400 men of the 1st Commando Brigade who waded ashore with him were killed, but Bill came off Sword Beach and eventually out of the war unscathed.

But his bagpipes were not so lucky and took a hit from German fire power. Bill recalled how he was running for cover under fire, carrying his pipes by his side, when a German mortar shell exploded nearby.

He escaped without a scratch but his pipes were damaged when they were hit by shrapnel from the mortar round.

Even that did not stop him – he pulled out a spare set of pipes from his rucksack and carried on playing.

Bill was revisiting Normandy's Sword Beach as part of the D-Day 60th anniversary celebrations despite being confined to a wheelchair since suffering a stroke around a year ago.

French D-Day veterans persuaded him to make the trip with a carer, matron and driver from the Palm Court nursing home in Dawlish, the quiet south Devon seaside town where he has lived for 50 years.

In his room overlooking the Channel, he is surrounded by memorabilia, including an oil painting, accurately described to the artist, of him playing the pipes on Sword Beach.

The historic bagpipes he played on the invasion beach, together with his kilt, beret, sporran and dirk, are now in a special D-Day exhibit at Dawlish museum.

The pipes he played during the campaign which followed the landings are in a museum at Pegasus Bridge, over the Caen canal captured by airborne troops.

Bill, born in Canada to Scottish parents, was living in Glasgow when he joined the Cameron Highlanders at 18 and volunteered for the commandos because they were "exciting".

He recalled on the night before D-Day he was aboard a convoy of 22 landing craft and played his pipes while sailing.

They arrived off France around 4am and watched as Allied tanks which went ashore first were knocked out by enemy fire.

"We started to wade ashore and I began playing the pipes when the water was up to my knees.

"I was the only one playing in action," said Bill, piper to Lord Lovat, who led the commando brigade. He said Lord Lovat overruled a War Office ban on playing in action and told him to use the pipes.

"I was in front of the troops all the way," said Bill, recalling that one Royal Marine sergeant swore at him, saying his playing would "bring all the Germans to us".

"I played the whole day on the beach, up to Pegasus Bridge and beyond," said Bill, who initially saw three months of action after D-Day before being returned temporarily to the UK before taking part in the Dutch campaign.

Bill's invasion beach exploits were immortalised in the 60s film of the D-Day landings and Operation Overlord, *The Longest Day* – and his piping was on the sound track.

Bill does not play the pipes now because he is unable to use his right hand following his stroke.

"I had always played the pipes seven days a week, but I don't think I will ever play them again," he said.

PEACE AT LAST

The bells rang out in celebration all over Europe and they rang as loudly as anywhere throughout Scotland. Nobody could stop smiling. It was not just the securing of victory but the fact that it was all over and people could walk the streets in safety once more, their loved ones no longer at risk, the light back on in their lives as well as in their houses.

The German surrender was officially signed at General Eisenhower's headquarters in France – a schoolroom in Rheims – in the early hours of Monday, May 7 1945. To be precise the time was 2.41am. Hostilities finally ended at one minute after midnight on May 8. With the Allies having made such advances and Germany having taken such a pounding and perhaps, most importantly, with Adolf Hitler, the inspiration behind the war, now dead, it was considered to be only a matter of time before the last all-clear was heard.

When the news finally broke through, the party began even though heavy rain was falling over much of Britain. In towns, cities and villages all over the country people gathered in groups and crowds. They just wanted to be with each other and the normal reserve gave way to hugs, kisses and back-slapping. This was VE Day and, even though there was still war raging in the Far East, the nightly worry about bombings was over.

The King broadcast the news to the Empire, as it was then known, and Churchill then addressed Parliament and the rest of the world, explaining the events that had led to the end of the conflict. He was driven to Buckingham Palace where he appeared on the balcony along with the royal family. Tens if not hundreds of thousands packed into the area to share their celebrations with the King, the Queen and their two daughters. Princess Elizabeth appeared in her army uniform. Later, she and Princess Margaret donned ordinary clothes and joined the crowds partying in the streets.

Later Churchill went to the Ministry of Health in Whitehall and from the balcony there he addressed the nation once more.

"God bless you all," he said. "This is your victory. It is the victory of the cause of freedom in every land."

In Scotland the celebrations were at least as joyful and noisy as everywhere else. In Glasgow street parties broke out with everyone delving into their ration-conscious larders to produce sandwiches, cakes, biscuits and, of course, a bottle or two. The pubs flung open their doors. Would they dare keep them closed? In Edinburgh the story was much the same with vast crowds gathering around the famous castle which had seen so many times of both war and peace. In Aberdeen street parties broke out all over the city but there were also throngs at the *Press & Journal* offices to buy newspapers as they came off the presses, hungry to read the news with their own eyes and perhaps collect a souvenir of the day that fear was expelled from their hearts.

All over Scotland bonfires were lit in celebration of the day the lights went back on.

It seemed that it was all over and soon the rationing would end and everything would get back to normal. It was a nice idea but for some life would never be normal again because there were empty seats at the dinner table and also, while the threat on the home front might have subsided, World War Two was still raging as Japan made its own attempt at world supremacy. Many families in Scotland still awaited news of their husbands, fathers, sons who were last heard of in Burma, Singapore, Malaya or other parts of the Far East which had previously only been given a passing mention in school geography lessons.

There were many tales of horror seeping back to Britain, stories of atrocities in prisoner-of-war camps in which little respect was shown for age or gender.

The world now concentrated on what was happening in that part of the world. It was no easy task to fight the Japanese in the jungles and there were as many tales of defeat as of victory. Something else was developing though – a bomb like no other and it was that bomb which finally ended World War Two. The morals of dropping such devastating bombs on Hiroshima and Nagasaki have been debated ever since but history recalls that it was all too much for ambitious Emperor Hirohito and the Japanese people and surrender was offered immediately.

Victory over Japan Day was August 15 and once again the parties burst out onto the streets.

World War Two really was over at last and the pipers sounded a lament for those who had been lost.

It had been the best of times as people rallied together to face down a common enemy and revealed bravery beyond what might have been expected. But it had been the worst of times with homes and families shattered forever by mankind's abuse of fellow man.

BLACK & WHITE
It's the Scotch!

The Press and Journal

No. 28,290, 198th Year. 1½d.

MONDAY, SEPTEMBER 3, 1945

A KEMSLEY NEWSPAPER

PEACE OVER WHOLE WORLD AFTER SIX YEARS' WAR

Mission Has Been Completed, MacArthur Declares

TOKIO BAY SURRENDER

WORLD PEACE WAS RESTORED AT EIGHTEEN MINUTES PAST ONE YESTERDAY MORNING.

General MacArthur, Supreme Allied Commander in the Pacific, pronounced the Japanese surrender proceedings closed.

Signature of the surrender documents by Japanese and Allied representatives was completed in eighteen minutes.

Thus ended the Second World War, and the world's first total war, almost six years to the day after it began with the German attack on Poland on September 1, 1939.

Winding up the solemn proceedings, General MacArthur said:—

"The guns are silent. A great tragedy has ended. A great victory has been won.

"The skies no longer rain death, the seas bear only commerce, men everywhere walk upright in the sunlight, the entire world lives quietly at peace.

"The holy mission has been completed, and in reporting this to you, the people, I speak for thousands of silent lips forever stilled among jungles and beaches and in deep waters of the Pacific which marked the way.

"I speak for the unnamed brave millions who are homeward bound to take up the challenge of that future which they did so much to salvage from the brink of disaster. A new era is upon us."

Black Armada Heightens Drama of Capitulation

From DAVID DIVINE
"The Press and Journal" War Correspondent
U.S.S. Missouri, Sunday.

AS Mamoru Shigemitsu, Foreign Minister of Japan and delegate of Emperor Hirohito, affixed his signature to the instrument of surrender, the first ship of the vast line of more than fifty transports carrying the Occupation Army—grim, dark, black as the ... Commodore Perry, ninety ...
Seldon ...

LUXURY IN PRISON CAMP

THERE are nineteen British airmen in an internment camp in Bangkok who will be almost sorry to leave. They live on a diet which includes chicken, roast beef, vegetables and eggs, and have not done one hour's work since they were interned.

Part of the time is spent in reading excellent books provided by their captors. They even managed to teach cricket to some American fliers in the camp.

The story of this life of luxury was told by six U.S. airmen, who looked anything but weak or maltreated, and have arrived in Calcutta from the camp. The reason for the kindness—the airmen were interned by the Siamese, who hated the Japs.

8-Point Surrender Terms

The text of the surrender document signed in Tokio by the Japanese and counter-signed by representatives ...

THE King, seated beside the Queen, driving by car from Crathie Church after the service yesterday. In front are the Princesses.

U.S. HELD V-DAY QUIETLY

MOST of the men of the U.S. Forces will return to civil life as soon as transport can bring them home, said President Truman in a broadcast early to-day.

"The high tide of victory will carry us forward to great achievements in the era which lies ahead, but we can perform them only in a world which is free from the threat of war.

"We depend on you who have known war in all its horror to keep this nation aware that only through co-operation among all the nations can any nation remain wholly secure," the President said addressing Servicemen.

"The other United Nations are as determined as we are that war must be abolished from the earth, as we know it, is to remain. Civilisation cannot survive another total war."

Americans took in their stride yesterday their official Victory ... Tru-

MINESWEEPERS BEGIN TASK

Clearing the Route to Singapore

BRITISH officers have been parachuted into Singapore, and S.E.A.C. was heard broadcasting instructions to them last night.

The main British landing at Singapore is expected for several days.

Minesweepers have been steadily clearing southwards through the Malacca Straits since yesterday. Convoys are waiting to sail in their wake.

British detachment ... officers ... reported to ... Georgetown, ... miles north ...

RUSSIANS ... ALL SAF... AND KU...

GENERALISSIMO ... a surprise speech ... sian people yesterday ... cow radio, announced ... and the Kurile Islan... Northern Pacific.

These territories wer... Japan after her "Pearl... at Port Arthur during ... Japanese war in 1904.

"We have our own s... to settle with Jap... before outlining th... aggression ... declared ... from ...

MYSTERY MESSAGE FROM FAR EAST

A MYSTERY message from the Far East may turn out to be good news for Mr and Mrs W Marsh, 62 Skene Street, Aberdeen.

Over the week-end Cable and Wireless officials were trying to locate a "Mrs Naish" to whom the cable was addressed at "62 Kent Street, Scotland."

It brought the news that a soldier named "Joseph Mason" is safe and well in Allied hands.

Having tried without success every Kent Street, and many others with similar names, the cable authorities sent out a call through the "Sunday Mail" for a claimant for the message.

Mr and Mrs Marsh saw the newspaper report, and last night they were trying to get in touch with the cable company in the belief that the message is from Mrs Marsh's son.

"I think the message will prove to be from my stepson, Gunner Joseph M'Sloy Masson," Mr Marsh told "The Press and Journal" last night.

Gunner Masson had been in the Regular Army for seven years before the fall of Hong-Kong, where he was taken prisoner.

He was formerly a milk roundsman with the Northern Co-operative Society in Aberdeen.

Cable from Australia

Among the first Aberdeen men to send word that they have been freed from the Japanese is Captain John W. Gardiner, Merchant Navy, 17 Oakhill Road.

In a telegram to his wife ... that he is well and is in Melbourne, Australia. He hopes to b...

... er has been ... three and ...

MR CHURCHILL IN ITALY

MR CHURCHILL, travelling under ... pseudonym which ca... be revealed, is touring No... Italy.

Accompanied ... his daughter, he arrived ... on Saturday night for a ... holiday in a U.S. Flying ... made a brief tour of ... light of the ... who cheered as hi...

Mr Churchill ... Field-Marshal ... will shun full ... views and p... Italian and Alli...

He will spen... golf and probab... villa in the Lak...

Russia to C... a F...

The U.S.S.R. is to ... with a whole fleet ... ly armed and equ... ing a destroye... of... a Polic... Warsaw R...